IN THE DAYS OF NOAH

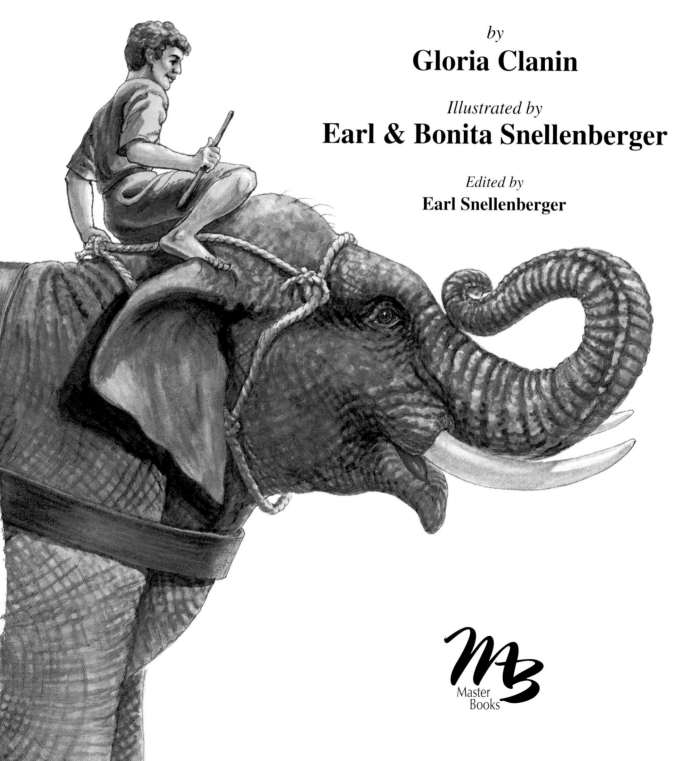

by
Gloria Clanin

Illustrated by
Earl & Bonita Snellenberger

Edited by
Earl Snellenberger

Master Books

First printing, October 1996
Second printing, March 1999

Copyright © 1996 by Master Books.

For information write: Master Books, P.O. Box 727, Green Forest, AR 72638.

ISBN: 0-89051-205-1

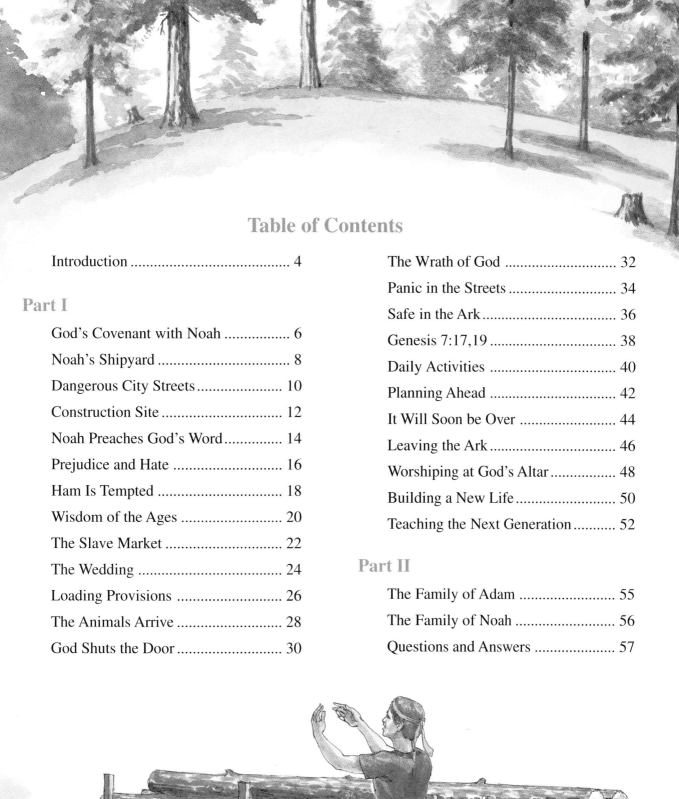

Table of Contents

Introduction

No other part of the Bible has received as much criticism and ridicule as the biblical account of God's judgment on a sin-filled earth and the resulting global flood.

Today, school children are taught to laugh at such a ridiculous story. Even children in many churches are told the Flood didn't cover the whole world, that it was just a local flood that affected only one area of the planet.

This book, *In the Days of Noah*, totally refutes such thinking! The Holy Bible is the inspired word of God and everything related in it is true. *In the Days of Noah* is based upon the Bible and faith in its accuracy.

However, even people who believe the story of Noah's ark have questions. How could Noah capture animals from all over the world to take with him? How could two of every animal in the world, and as many as seven of some, fit in the ark? How could only eight people feed and care for thousands of animals? This book was written to help answer such questions. A fictional story based on facts, found in Part I, will answer some questions. Part II contains explanations of many things that were common knowledge in Noah's time—such as the length of a cubit, or the birth order of Noah's sons (page 57). Part II also presents technical and scientific information about the Flood.

Some questions people have about Noah's ark and the Flood have arisen because of misconceptions and misrepresentations. For example, we have all seen the charming children's books that picture a quaint Noah's ark—with a giraffe sticking its head out of a window. This, however, does not even begin to show the enormous size of the ark and the magnitude of the incredible events that occurred on earth during the time of Genesis 6–9. These four chapters tell of God's power, righteousness, and provision for the eight people left in the world who trusted in Him.

It is also the record of a world filled with people who hated God and worshiped idols they had made with their own hands. They rejected God and the love He wanted to give them. Psalm 9:15–16 is a description of what happens when men run their own lives apart from God.

> The heathen are sunk down in the pit that they made: in the net which they hid is their own foot taken. The Lord is known by the judgment which He executeth; the wicked is snared in the work of his own hands.

God is a loving God, but He is also a holy and righteous God. Although sin cannot remain unpunished, God prefers to show mercy and forgiveness. Jonah 4:2 says, "Thou art a gracious God, and merciful, slow to anger, and of great kindness." The Bible tells us God prefers mercy to judgment.

As terrible as the destruction of the world by the Flood was, we know that God is patient as well as just. God gave mankind every opportunity to repent *before* He sent the Flood. Noah was a "preacher of righteousness" (2 Pet. 2:5). He was God's witness for hundreds of years with no

converts but his own family. Yes, Noah no doubt preached for many, many years! The Bible tells us that Noah lived to be 950 years old.

Most people do not realize how very different the earth was before the Flood. It was normal for people to live for hundreds of years. And there possibly was no rain until the Flood, "but there went up a mist from the earth, and watered the whole face of the ground" (Gen. 2:6). The rivers were fed by artesian wells, plant life was lush and abundant, and there was probably just one large continent instead of several. The mountains were most likely rolling hills compared to what we see now. It would have taken far less water to cover the highest mountains at the time of the Flood than it would today. You will find out more about these things in Part II.

We would have liked it if Noah had given us more specific information about the events leading up to, during, and after the Flood. Since he did not, Bible-believing scientists have sought to fill in the gaps. And authors interested in their research and findings have written books such as this one. Perhaps the details that related to the Flood were not as important to Noah as mankind's continuing rejection of God and the coming judgment.

The Bible has not told us specifically what Noah did for a living, but Genesis 9:20 does tell us he was "a man of the soil" later in life. In this Bible-based story, we have made him the wealthy owner of a large ship building company who also owns vast forests and farmlands. It seems logical to assume that God would have given Noah all the resources he needed to accomplish His will.

Staying faithful to the information the Bible does tell us, we have filled in other blanks. Also, we have filled out the very basic and brief biblical story, giving names to Noah's wife and daughters-in-law and including some fictional characters.

While some things were very different before the Flood, other things were very much the same as they are today. Jesus Christ said that before His second coming it would be, once again, as it was before the Flood. When people turn their backs on our loving God, they open themselves up to evil. Jesus said, "as it was in the Days of Noah, so shall it be also in the days of the Son of man" (Luke 17:26).

Looking at the world we live in today, we see much of what it was like in the days just before the Flood. There is a widespread disbelief in God, wars, gang violence, liberal court systems, lack of respect for human life, rise in spiritism, the list goes on and on. Reading a newspaper or watching the news on television confirms the reality of evil in the world. But we are not left without hope. That hope is in Jesus Christ who knew it would once again be as it was *in the days of Noah.* And just as He did in Noah's day, He has provided us a way of salvation.

Part I
God's Covenant with Noah

Noah watched his sons bringing the elephants in for the noon break. He was proud of the fine men they were becoming. Lately, Noah often thought of his sons—and of the years ahead which he knew would be difficult for all of them. Fortunately, his was a close family, bound by their love of God and for each other. They would need the strength provided by these bonds.

Shem, the tallest of the three brothers, looked up and saw their father waiting for them under the shade tree on the rise. It was a rare treat for Noah to meet with his sons during the day. The family lands and business required much of his time.

Shem, Ham, and Japheth quickly dismounted their elephants and hurried to Noah. The day had grown unusually warm, and they were almost as eager to get in the shade as they were to see their father. They knew Noah had brought the noon meal with him. The three raced to see who could reach their father—and the food—first.

Ham had enjoyed helping Shem and Japheth that morning—and whenever he got the chance. Younger than his two brothers, he still spent most of each day at his studies. Ham felt something special was about to happen, for Noah ate hurriedly, hardly speaking to them. Father wasn't his usual calm self, and seemed impatient for them to finish eating.

As soon as the meal was over and the food put out of the way, Noah sat on a nearby bench. His sons gathered about him. Noah was now over 500 years old and there was some gray hair at his temples. But he had the appearance, strength, and energy of a much younger man. Noah looked intently at each one of his sons, then blurted out, "Tomorrow is the day we start work on the ark."

Noah's sons sat in stunned silence for a moment. Shem was the first to catch his father's excitement. He began asking Noah questions as fast as his quick mind formed them.

Noah raised his hands for silence and laughed at Shem's eagerness. "One question at a time, please. There is much to discuss and many plans to be made. But before the true work can begin, we need to go to God in prayer."

Noah bowed his head and spoke, "Lord God, You are the one who has made everything there is; the heavens and the earth and all that is in them. You rule in power and wisdom, and know all things. Your heart is deeply grieved by the evil that is present on earth. Guide us to do Your will. Lord, as we begin construction on the ark, we ask for Your blessing. Give us the strength and knowledge to accomplish this great work to Your glory and honor."

As Noah looked up and saw the intense expressions on his son's faces, he wondered if they were able to grasp the difficulty of the task ahead. He knew the hatred they would face by obeying God in a world that seemed to grow more violent each year. "Sons, years ago I was met with silence each time I stood before the people and told them of God's coming judgment. As years went by, the crowds began to ridicule and mock me."

Noah wanted to be certain his sons understood how the evil started and why God could not let it continue. "Your great-grandfather Methuselah has told you about the things that happened at the beginning. How God created a perfect and beautiful world and filled it with life—in the sea, the air, and on the land. Then He created the first two people, Adam and Eve, and placed them in a magnificent garden. He provided everything they needed to live a wonderful, happy life. God told them they could eat anything they wanted in the garden except for the fruit of one tree, the tree of the knowledge of good and evil.

"Later, the evil one, who hated God and all He had created, appeared to Eve in the form of a serpent. He caused her to doubt the reason behind God's command not to eat the forbidden fruit. God had said that to eat of the tree would bring death. But the evil one told Eve if she ate the fruit of the tree she would not die, but would become a god, too.

"Eve listened to her own heart and desires and did not turn to God for wisdom. She took a bite of the fruit and gave it to Adam who also ate of it. Mankind had chosen to ignore God's will. Rebellion and self-will—and death—had entered the world.

"Since then, the wickedness of man has grown greater with each passing year. Those of us who still trust in the Lord God have tried to warn people that the wicked are following the evil one who deceived Adam and Eve. But they do not want to listen and grow even angrier. In fact, I believe our lives may be in danger some day.

"As you know, God told me to build an ark while I continued to warn others that He is going to destroy this sin-filled earth. We now have enough cured gopher wood to begin the ark's construction.

"Sons, all three of you will be helping to build the ark. And I want you with me tomorrow when I show the plans for the ark to Jabez and tell him it will be built in the great clearing behind our home. As head of my shipyard, Jabez will be involved in all phases of the construction. Can you imagine the look of surprise on his face! Sons, this is something I don't want you to miss."

Noah's Shipyard

Noah, this is gigantic!" Jabez gasped. He stared in amazement at the carefully drawn plans on the parchment Noah had rolled out before him. "It's a full 300 cubits long. Nothing this enormous has ever been built before."

"Yes, Jabez, you're absolutely right," said Noah, nodding in agreement with his astonished shipyard foreman. "The ark will be colossal! But, then, God has mighty plans in mind for its use. Years ago, when God told me I was to build it, I felt humbled at first by the scale of the project."

"Humbled?" Jabez responded. "I'm overwhelmed! To build this ark, we would need ten shipyards the size of this one. And even if we had the room to construct it, where would we find enough seasoned gopher wood?"

"Jabez, calm down. These are not problems," soothed Noah. "For many years I have been collecting great amounts of gopher wood. It has been stacked and aging at the edge of my forest. Remember? You saw some of it years ago. When you asked what it was for, I told you it was for God's work. The ark has been the reason for my years of labor—and for the work of my sons when they grew old enough to help. The ark is to be built in the great clearing behind my home."

Jabez couldn't believe his ears! Had Noah lost his mind? All that religion must have done funny things to his head.

"Noah, think about what you are saying," Jabez said, facing Noah again and trying to keep his voice calm. "How do you plan to launch the ark? It would be impossible to move. And the clearing is far above sea level and some distance from the coast."

Jabez, we won't have to move the ark. The water will come to it."

"Noah, be reasonable. Water has never flowed uphill, and it certainly doesn't come down from the sky."

"Jabez, please have some faith. I don't know how God is going to do it, but the sea will completely overflow the land. And, though it has never happened before, water will fall from the sky

above as well. God will bring a great flood that will destroy mankind and all land animals. Everyone and any animal not in the ark will die. The ark has to be immense. It will carry a male and female of every kind of animal in the world to preserve God's creation. There must also be space to store food for all of them."

"Yes, I see there's room enough," observed Jabez, looking at the ark's plans again. "I see it is to be three stories tall. We have no equipment that will raise the heavy beams high enough."

"That is a problem," Noah replied, stroking his beard. "Perhaps we will think of some way. . . ."

As Noah's voice trailed off, his thoughts were interrupted by Ham. "Father, I have an idea. I believe I can figure out a way to raise the beams. The method we use here in the shipyard can be modified to build a huge crane. And if we add elephant power, I'm certain it would work!"

Noah smiled fondly at his youngest son. There was pride in his voice when he said to Jabez, "I can never figure out where this boy gets all of his ideas. God has truly blessed him with an inventive mind. And don't you see, Jabez, together—and with God's guidance—we will find an answer to every problem."

"Noah, I see that you are determined to build the ark. I also see you have three fine sons to help you," Jabez observed. "And, of course, you also have me. I still don't understand all this, but I'm willing to do what you want."

Noah had somehow known that Jabez hadn't really been listening all those times he had told him about the coming judgment. "The ark that we are going to build," he told Jabez, "is God's plan to save all who turn to Him and trust Him. God will keep everyone who is inside safe from destruction. That includes you and your family. I want all of you to be there with us, my friend."

"Noah, I appreciate your concern for me and my family. And I know you are convinced that building the ark is God's will. I wish I had your faith. But let's talk more of this later. Right now I need to ask a favor of your sons."

"How can we help you?" Japheth eagerly asked.

"As you know, my wife Huldah is a wonderful cook. When your father told me that you would be coming in to the shipyard with him today, I asked her to prepare a special noon meal for all of us. Would the three of you go to my home and escort my daughter Lea back to the shipyard? She will be bringing the food and serving it, but I don't want her to come here alone."

"I'll go for Lea," cried Ham. "And I don't need any company!"

Ham was turning to leave when Noah called to him, "Ham, we appreciate your willingness to be helpful, but I want your brothers to go with you."

Frowning, Ham stopped and waited for Japheth and Shem.

"I know you would rather walk Lea here by yourself, Ham, but the city streets are too dangerous," advised Shem. "The street gangs think nothing of attacking un-guarded adults in the center of the city. And, who knows, maybe there will be so much food Japheth and I will have to help you carry it."

Noah watched his sons leave, then turned to Jabez. "The more the Nephilim come from Nod to our city, the more our problems increase. What a tribe of cruel giants they are! And their master, the evil one, is using them to corrupt the daughters of men. The drugs they sell destroy our children's minds and encourage crime. It amuses them to see our young people die or be involved in senseless violence."

"You're right, Noah. But, what can be done? Well, I need to get my crew to finish the deck of this ship," Jabez declared as he walked away.

Dangerous City Streets

We'll save time if we go down this side street," shouted Japheth above the noise of the marketplace crowd.

"Right," said Shem, as he followed Japheth around a corner. "We don't want that delicious food to get cold." He sniffed the air to savor the good smells coming from the baskets Ham and Lea, who walked behind them, were carrying.

Japheth looked at Shem and questioned, "I wonder if Lea is learning to cook like her mother?"

Shem laughed, "She had better do so if she wants to impress Ham, since his favorite thing in life is eating." Ham and Lea, deep in conversation, didn't hear a word his brothers were saying.

Suddenly, without warning, a street gang burst from a dark alleyway and rushed toward them.

The three brothers and Lea backed up to a wall as they were surrounded. The gang members pulled out weapons as they moved in closer.

"Well, look who we have here," taunted the gang leader. " The high and mighty sons of the rich preacher Noah and a pretty little friend. Got any of the crazy old man's money on you?"

"We don't want any trouble with you," said Shem, drawing himself up to his full height.

"You got trouble when you set foot on our territory," snarled the gang leader. "You and your brothers think you're too good to party with the likes of us or visit the temples at festival time. But I'll bet you'd like to party with us," he said, smirking at Lea. "I've got something that will

make you feel real good, and I can show you how to have fun." The boy held out a pouch of powder to Lea who moved behind Ham's protective arm.

"You can be arrested for having those drugs on you," said Japheth.

"Worried about me, are you?" the leader laughed sarcastically. "Don't bother! I always have enough money to bribe some official, or I tell the judge a sad story and he lets me go. I've never spent more than two days in jail. So, if your little girlfriend doesn't want anything from me, how about the three of you giving us some. . . ."

At that moment a group of city security soldiers noticed what was happening and ran into the side street. The gang ran off and quickly disappeared into a dark alley

"You're lucky we came by on patrol," said the officer in charge as he studied the brothers and Lea. "Aren't you Noah's sons?"

The three nodded in response. "What are you doing in this part of town without a guard?" the officer questioned.

"Our father sent us to escort our friend Lea to the shipyard," answered Japheth.

"I asked why you boys are here without a hired guard?" the officer continued. "Your father is a rich man. Why didn't he send guards with you for protection? Does he think that the God he is always ranting about will take care of you? We'll see you safely to your father's shipyard, but don't come here alone again."

The sullen security soldiers escorted the silent group back to the shipyard. Their commanding officer thought that since Noah was a wealthy man he could cause trouble for him. He wanted no harm to come to Noah's sons and the girl in the area his forces patrolled.

Construction Site

Father, I thought after all these years of work on the ark we would be much further along! How many years will it take?" Shem said, exasperation in his voice. He stood with Noah on the lower level of their home's garden where they had a clear view of the entire massive frame of the ark.

Noah sighed and looked at his son. "Shem, I know you are impatient to move on to the next stages of preparation, but this is God's work, and it will take exactly as long as God wills. I wish we could work on the ark full-time, but we all have our jobs to do at the shipyard as well. Progress has been slow, but its construction must be flawless. And think, with each passing year, God is giving men more time to repent of their sinful ways and turn to Him. We should be grateful that He is such a merciful God.

Nearby, Japheth was talking to Sarene. She was slim, with dark, waist-length hair. Sarene was like a sister to Noah's sons, for their parents had been close friends for many years. Her father had been Noah's distant cousin. Two months before, Sarene's parents had been robbed and murdered on the way to visit her grandparents.

Sarene stood so she could look at Shem as he talked to his father. Shem had always been like a big brother to her. But now that he was a grown man, Sarene noticed how strong and handsome he had become. *Of all Noah's sons, Shem is most like him — in word and deed,* she thought. *And with that newly-grown beard, he even looks most like his father.* Sarene wondered if Shem would mind if she sat and talked with him after the evening meal.

Japheth's voice interrupted her thoughts, "I know how you must feel, with your parents gone, Sarene. But we know that no matter what happens, we can trust God, even though we don't understand why certain things happen."

"It's been very difficult. I miss them so," Sarene responded. " Without God's sustaining love and your family, I don't know what I would do."

"Sarene, we're your family now. You can depend on us. When it is time for the tax collectors to come and go over your father's accounts, my father

wants to be with you to make sure they treat you fairly. Father believes the city officials and tax collectors are no better than thieves. They would love to get their hands on your father's money and lands. Let my father know when your parents' estate is to be settled."

Sarene quietly replied, "I would like that. Noah has been so good to me. I don't understand why the people in the city are angry with him. I'm even afraid for his safety. I hear them talking about him everywhere I go. He has never done anything bad to any of them. In fact, he has helped many of them and often gives money whenever he hears of a need. Why are they so angry about his preaching and the ark?"

Japheth shrugged his shoulders and answered her, "Father is only telling them what God has instructed him to say. They are angry because what he is telling them shows them how sinful their lives are. They don't want to hear it. They wish he would go away and leave them alone."

Noah Preaches God's Word

God loves you. He doesn't want anyone to perish," Noah shouted, trying to be heard above those who jeered him. The crowd had grown increasingly restless. *Perhaps it's because we're so near the new temple,* thought Noah.

Be quiet, Preacher Man, and go away," a woman yelled. "You're going to make the temple priests and guards—and the sea gods—angry!"

"Are you afraid they will see you listening to me? You have nothing to fear from the golden idols of the so-called gods of the sea," responded Noah, pointing to the temple behind him. "They were made by the hands of man and have no power. You should fear neither idols nor giants nor any man. Rather, fear the Lord God of heaven who will someday destroy this wicked world with a cleansing flood."

A man in the back of the crowd snorted, "What makes you think the waters of the sea will rise up and flood the earth in the future? That's never happened before. Things have always been as they are now, and will always be the same."

Noah turned to the man and pleaded, "Please believe me. It isn't what I think, but what God says! He will judge the earth, but you can escape destruction. You have *chosen* to worship power-less idols, and you have given the priests the power to control you. You allow them to take your money and force your daughters to serve in their temples. Is this really what you want for yourselves and your children? What if it's your daughter they want next year for the sacrifice?" Noah questioned, pointing to a man near him.

"No, no! I don't want my daughter sacrificed, but what can I do? What can we do?" he said.

"You can turn to God," declared Noah. "The Lord God is the one and only true God. Only He, the Creator of this world and everything in it, has the right to be worshiped. Because of His love for you, He has warned you of His coming judgment. He wants you to turn to Him and leave your idols. He is a just God and will honor your repentance."

Several people in the crowd were swayed by the things Noah said. Was it possible there really was only one true God? And if so, perhaps the coming judgment was real. Noah certainly believed it. He had told them there would be room for all of them on the ark he was building.

"Don't listen to him," yelled a man in a red tunic. He shook his fist and screamed at Noah, "We can do whatever we want. What's right for you doesn't mean it's right for anyone else. Leave us alone!"

Those in the crowd who had been touched by what Noah said remained silent. But as they looked at the shouting people all around them, they began to worry. What would my friends and family think if I believed? Would they laugh at me? Would I lose my job? No, there was too much at stake to side with Noah.

In a window overlooking the crowd, a woman watched the scene below. She had sent her slave to alert the temple guards. That man Noah should be locked up. How dare he say those things about her gods. That god of Noah wouldn't let anyone have a good time. Why would anybody want to follow a god like that? *Noah should be stopped so he doesn't confuse people,* she thought. Looking in the direction of the temple, she saw the priests and temple guards running down the steps.

Shem, at the base of the platform saw them, too. He knew the priests would seek to have the angry mob harm his father. Noah felt a hard tug on his robe and looked down. He saw the look of alarm on Shem's face and knew it was time to leave. Noah leapt down, and they quickly escaped. The two ducked into one side street, then another, and disappeared into the marketplace.

When they were back safely at their home, Noah praised God and thanked Him for protecting them. Preaching God's word was becoming more dangerous with each passing day, but he would never stop doing it. Next week he would go to the distant land of Nod to preach again, and Shem would accompany him.

Prejudice and Hate

Noah's wife, Rebecca, accompanied by her bodyguard, stopped at a marketplace stall and greeted the owner's daughter. "Good morning, Rachel. I've heard you have some beautiful new fabrics from Nod. I'd like to see them."

Rachel quickly brought out several brightly colored patterns. And after telling Rebecca about the fabrics, she shyly asked, "How is your son Japheth? I haven't seen him around the marketplace with his brothers lately."

"He's just fine, thank you. Japheth has been working on the ark and hasn't been in the city recently," Rebecca replied. She smiled, realizing her handsome, rusty-haired son had caught Rachel's attention.

As Rebecca looked at the fabrics, two women and their bodyguard stopped on the other side of the street. The women glared at Rebecca, as if offended by her presence. Then one, dressed in yellow, turned to her companion and spoke in a loud voice—for she wanted Rebecca to hear.

"Look, there's mad Noah's wife, Rebecca, buying fabrics. She can well afford them, for her deranged husband *refused* to pay the new voluntary temple tax that all decent citizens willingly pay. He won't contribute so we can have another beautiful new temple to worship in, but he has money to spare when it comes to building that monstrous ark."

"And look at her," said the woman in red pointing in Rebecca's direction. "She hangs on to the old ways and looks down on us because we do not. She thinks she's too good to attend the plays and lectures. Well, better to be open to new ideas than to have a closed mind like her. Even the judge's wife attends meetings to contact the spirit beings and the dead. Noah says they are demons and will harm us. What does he know?"

Rebecca's guard turned his back to the women so he could pretend he didn't hear them. If Noah didn't pay so well, he wouldn't be seen with the wife of a crazy man.

The woman in yellow continued the verbal assault. "Noah's family refused to come to the new temple festival for the sacrifice of the maiden. Don't they care if we have good fortune next year? Something should be done about them."

Rachel, embarrassed for Rebecca, stepped nearer and whispered, "I'm sure your God will protect you and your family." Being so close to her, Rebecca noticed marks on Rachel's arms.

"Thank you, Rachel. He will. But how did you get all those terrible bruises?" Rebecca softly asked. Rachel looked down and turned away in an effort to hide her arms. She shrank from Rebecca's gentle touch on her shoulder.

When Rachel finally turned around to face Rebecca, there were tears in her eyes. "One day last week very few shoppers came to the market-

place, and I only sold one piece of cloth. My father was very angry and said if I had tried harder I could have sold much more. He said I deserved to be punished. He doesn't try to hurt my brother, who's older, anymore, but he often beats me if I do not sell enough to suit him."

"Rachel, would you want to come to work for me and live in my home?" asked Rebecca. "I promise you would *never* be beaten again. If you want to come with me, please go tell your father I wish to speak to him."

Rachel was gone in an instant, and returned with her father. Rebecca spoke to him of her need for a new handmaid. And when Rebecca told him of the generous sum of money he would receive from Noah each month for Rachel's work, he readily agreed to her employment. Rachel could not believe her good fortune. She had never dared dream of anything this wonderful. No one had ever been so kind to her before.

Ham Is Tempted

Noah and Jabez stood in the midday sun at the shipyard, looking at the fishing vessel under construction. "Ham has not come back to the shipyard after lunch," Jabez told Noah. "This is the third time this week. I do not know where he has gone, but when he is not here the men on his crew do not work as hard."

Noah went to the shipyard office and asked Shem and Japheth to find Ham and bring him back with them. As soon as they were outside, Japheth told Shem he thought he knew where their younger brother was. One of the workmen had told Japheth he had seen Ham going in the drinking house on the south side of the docks. And he hadn't known whether or not to tell Noah.

The two brothers walked quickly to the drinking house. When they entered it, Japheth was the first to see Ham in the dim light. "There he is, Shem. He's sitting with his back turned to us."

Shem looked to where Japheth pointed, saw Ham, and then saw the two Nephilim. One was busy threatening a man and demanding his money. The other seemed lost in his drink and the woman by his side. Shem hoped the trouble-making giants wouldn't notice them.

Japheth and Shem went over to Ham and stood next to him. Ham, unhappy to see them, said

in annoyance. "Hello, brothers. Are you here to tell me how to live my life again?"

Japheth turned to the woman sitting next to Ham and said coldly, "Please leave!" She glared at Japheth as she stood up and went to another table. "Ham, what are you doing in a place like this?" Shem said in a low voice.

"I work hard for my money and I'll spend it anyway I please! If I want to have some fun and spend a little time with a pretty girl, what's wrong with that?" snarled Ham. He was tired of everyone telling him what to do.

"The women here don't care about you, just the money you bring. Are you blinded to the danger here? Even the music in this place is against God," Japheth observed.

Then Shem continued, "This is known to be a Nephilim hangout. I've heard rumors that men come in here and have drugs slipped in their drinks—and they are never seen again. Perhaps they end up as slaves, beaten and worked to death in some remote, hidden Nephilim gold mine."

Ham looked uncomfortable. He lowered his head and mumbled, "I can take care of myself."

Japheth shook his head and pleaded, "God has picked you to go on the ark. Do you still want to? You have to make a choice, Ham. You either walk with the Lord God *or* the evil one."

Ham knew the truth of what Japheth was saying. Even though Ham knew he was in the wrong, he wasn't sure he wanted to give up his friends.

Shem saw the indecision in Ham's face. "Please, come with us! Look around you. Are these the people you want to be identified with?

Ham stood to leave with his brothers, and suddenly felt dizzy. He realized he had been drugged. Shem and Japheth each grabbed an arm to steady him, and the three brothers quickly left.

One of the Nephilim watched them leave, an angry scowl on his face. The strong young man would have brought him a good price from the slave traders at the next port.

Wisdom of the Ages

A few days after his brothers had taken him from the drinking house, Ham sat on the wall of his father's garden. The evening meal was over and it was time to relax from the day's labors. He had spent a lot of time thinking about the things Japheth and Shem had said. He realized how easily he had begun thinking the way his friends did. Only now, he understood that they had never really been true friends at all. What if his brothers hadn't come looking for him? God had saved him from a terrible fate. Ham knew he had an important decision to make.

His great-grandfather Methuselah and grandfather Lamech had joined them for the evening meal. It was always a special treat for the family when they came. Everyone was very busy, and there never seemed to be enough time to get together as often as they would have liked.

As Rebecca brought a dessert of fruit and pastries for her family, everyone praised her for the wonderful meal she had served. She laughed and said, "With your appetites, I could serve you baked straw and you wouldn't notice." But Rebecca was pleased her family had noticed her efforts and she sang all the way back to the kitchen.

Ham was eager to hear one of the stories he knew Methuselah would tell. His father Enoch had been very close to Adam, so he knew many wonderful stories about the early days.

Tonight, Methuselah looked weary. "As far as I know, only a handful of people in all the world still believe in the Lord God," he sighed. "There is evidence of it everywhere you go. Today I was in the market place and all around me everyone was yelling and swearing at each other. Customers were screaming that they had been overcharged and merchants were screaming back. Soldiers were shoving their way though the crowds with no respect for anyone. Even the children were loud, demanding their parents obey them. Everywhere I looked, I saw and heard anger and violence.

"It grieves the Lord God to see people behave like this," Methuselah said. "This is not the world He designed in the beginning. Adam told my father about the beautiful garden God

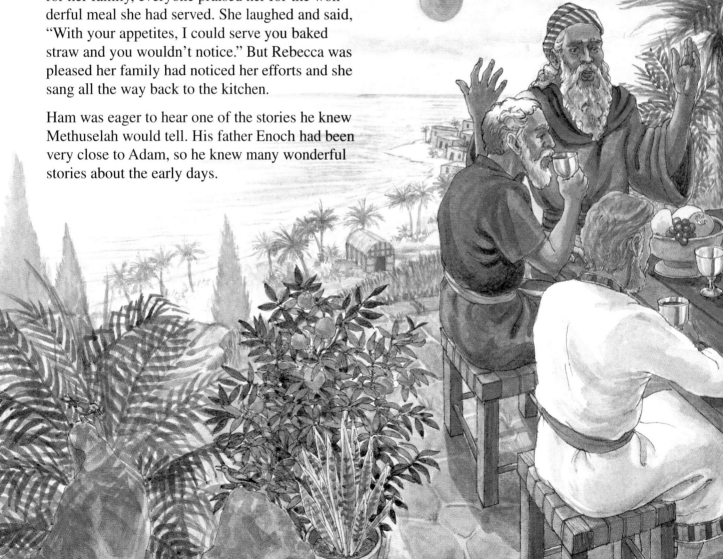

planted. He said there is nothing today to compare to its beauty.

"The animals were all friendly and enjoyed being around them. The beautiful tigers and lions would seek them out to be petted. There was no fear, and everywhere you looked there was food to eat. Every day was filled with wonderful new things to see and experience.

"Then came the awful day the evil one appeared to Eve as a snake. She listened to him instead of God, and ate the fruit of the tree of knowledge of good and evil. Adam followed her in rebellion to God and ate of the tree, too. The world was forever changed.

"All of Adam and Eve's lives they mourned the evil they saw around them. When Cain killed his brother Abel, they fully realized for the first time that their sin would be carried on in their children. As the population grew, it was obvious that the children of Cain were evil and lusted after power and riches. Adam and Eve often wished they could go back and undo what they had done. It had seemed like such a small thing at the time. What could taking one small bite hurt? They had not realized that their actions would live on in the lives of others."

As Ham listened to Methuselah, he felt touched by the wise old man's words. Ham closed his eyes and thought to himself, *How could I have been so foolish? I turned my back on God just like the rest of the world. I thought only of myself and what I wanted. Why didn't I listen to Father when he tried to warn me about my friends? I thought he was just old fashioned and didn't understand. I'm the one who didn't understand! They don't care about me, and those girls only care about having a good time. None are as kind and sweet as Lea. Please, God, forgive me. I've sinned against You and hurt those who love me. I want to change. Give me the strength to do Your will and be the man You want me to be.* When Ham opened his eyes, he looked at his family and thanked God for each of them.

The Slave Market

Japheth burst into the shipyard office and struggled to speak as he gasped for breath, "I just heard that Sarene was taken from her home before dawn and is to be sold at the slave market this morning. I ran as fast as I could to tell you."

Shem, standing next to Noah, spoke in a voice filled with alarm, "Father, we have to get there quickly. Someone may have bought her already. I pray we're not too late!"

Before Shem was even through speaking Noah had grabbed his money pouch. With his dear cousin dead, he thought of Sarene as his own daughter. His heart pounding, Noah ran out the door with a frantic Shem at his heels. Japheth, still trying to catch his breath, followed after them.

Shem led the way as they raced through the streets. They reached the slave market just as the weeping Sarene was led to the center of the platform. The slave trader cried out in a loud voice that caught everyone's attention, "Here is the daughter of one of your nobles who cheated the city of a lot of money. What am I bid for her?"

A Nephilim made the first offer. "I want that one! I will make her one of my wives," the brutal giant roared. Noah shouted out a counter-bid as he and Shem rushed toward the platform. Another man bid, then the Nephilim raised his offer.

Shem had never felt so much fear. Until now, he hadn't realized how much Sarene meant to him. He pleaded with Noah, "No matter what it takes, Father, you have to be high bidder." Noah assured Shem that no one would outbid him.

Sarene was a beautiful girl, and the bidding went higher and higher. In time, only Noah and the giant continued to bid against one another. Finally, the Nephilim bid no more. Noah's bid was high!

The Nephilim was furious. "Noah, mark my words. You will live to regret this moment!" He shook his fist at Noah, then turned on his heels and stomped away—vowing to seek revenge.

Those in the crowd thought this was most amusing. They jeered and laughed. High and mighty Noah has preached for years about how wrong it

was to have slaves. "Everyone is a relative," he had said. And here he was, buying the daughter of his cousin. What a hypocrite!

Noah turned to the crowd. "I have not bought Sarene to have as a slave, but to set her free. God created all men in His image and they are of equal value. No man has the right to own another."

Sarene ran down from the platform and into Noah's waiting arms. She told Noah how the tax collectors had appeared without warning that morning while it was still dark. They began removing everything and ordering the servants to leave. The officials lied and said her father had never paid his taxes and it would take every thing he had owned and more to pay the debt.

"They jailed me immediately, and later brought me to the slave market to be sold," Sarene explained. "I begged my servants to tell you what happened. I was so afraid you wouldn't know until too late. Thank God you came in time."

Sarene tearfully clung to Noah as he held her tenderly. Over her head he watched the relief on Shem's face. He had never seen his son so upset and emotional. Then Noah smiled to himself. He had thought of a way to keep Sarene safe and make his son very happy.

The Wedding

Methuselah stood proudly under the grape arbor. Family and friends sat on benches facing him, waiting for the wedding ceremony to start. He had performed many marriages in his lifetime, but this one was very special. Methuselah's thoughts were on Shem and Sarene as they approached him from opposite sides of the arbor. *They have been picked by God to be on the ark. This truly is a joyous time! Shem and Sarene will be the parents of a family in the new world,* he said to himself.

Methuselah placed his hand on their clasped hands and began, "And the Lord God said, 'It is not good for man to live alone; I will make him an help meet for him . . . and they shall be one flesh.' The Lord God planned for one man to be married to one woman that He might bless them and multiply them. The bond of marriage will strengthen so that you will be stronger together than each alone. Raise the children you are given to know and obey the Lord God. Teach them of all that has happened since the beginning that they might teach their children. Remain faithful to the Lord God and to each other, and God will bless you all the days of your lives."

Shem looked tenderly at Sarene, his heart filled with love for her. Again, he praised God that she did not fall into the hands of the wicked, but was now his wife. As for Sarene, she thanked God for blessing her with such a wonderful husband.

As Methuselah continued, Japheth leaned back and glanced behind his parents to see Rachel, only to find her looking back at him with a smile on her lips. For a minute he was embarrassed at having been caught, but then he thought, *Maybe she does care for me after all. I was afraid it was my imagination.* The wonderful day suddenly looked brighter still to Japheth.

Ham, sitting behind his parents, was politely listening to Jabez comment on the happy occasion. He would much rather be sitting next to Lea, but perhaps he could figure out a way to be near her at the marriage feast.

Lea's mother, Huldah, was closely watching everything. She had plans for Lea and Ham. Her husband was a master tradesman and was well-respected, but they were still far below Noah and Rebecca socially. If Lea married into Noah's family, perhaps they, too, would be accepted by the nobles of the city.

When the ceremony was over, Huldah whispered to Jabez, "Noah may be crazy, but he has power because of his money. Ham has become very responsible. He is ambitious and will one day be even richer than his father. You must speak to Noah soon about Lea. Do not let another family get ahead of us in arranging a marriage. Why should anyone else's daughter marry into such wealth?"

Rebecca was filled with joy after the ceremony. She had known for years how Sarene felt about Shem. Now Sarene was truly her daughter. Rebecca drew close to Noah and spoke, "Do not be surprised if there are soon two more weddings in the family. Ham has settled down and grown into a fine young man. He often goes to Jabez's house to discuss work, but I think the main reason is to see Lea. Japheth makes excuses to be in the same room with Rachel whenever he can. She is such a fine girl and truly has grown to love the Lord."

Noah smiled and put his arm around Rebecca. "If our sons are half as happy in marriage as we are, my dear wife, they will be happy indeed."

Loading Provisions

Noah climbed to the top of the discarded scaffold that had not been used since the ark's completion. He looked at the scene below him with a heavy heart.

The 50 years since Shem married Sarene had brought both joy and sorrow. There was great happiness in Noah's family when Shem's wedding was soon followed by Japheth's marriage to Rachel. And then, two years later Ham wed Lea. All three of his sons were now married to fine young women who loved the Lord.

The years had also brought sadness. Last week Noah had buried Methuselah, and he missed him very much. Noah had been close to his father, Lamech, but since his death seven years ago, he had become even closer to Methuselah. God had blessed Methuselah with 969 years of life in which to serve Him. Now God had given Methuselah rest.

Noah felt the scaffold shake beneath his feet as Shem climbed to join him. He turned to his son and said, "I was just thinking that all our godly ancestors are gone." Noah sighed, "Today, there may be only myself, Rebecca, my sons, and their wives in all the world that believe in God."

Shem placed his arm around his father. He knew how deeply Noah grieved. He turned and said, "Father, I know how difficult it has been for you. But I want you to know how proud I am to be your son. Your faithfulness to the commands of God have been an inspiration to our whole family. We have prayed that others would come to know the Lord, but they have not. No one can force another to love God; each person must make his own choice. You have been God's faithful witness, you have done all you could do."

"Perhaps when the animals arrive, people's hearts will be touched and finally some will believe," Noah said.

As they were speaking Ham appeared in the door of the ark. He was directing workmen as they stored the supplies. He had been working since before sunrise.

"Ham is doing a fine job of organizing the loading and storage of all we will need on the ark and in the new world," Shem told his father. "He has made careful lists of everything being loaded and exactly where it is being stored. That will be a big help to us once we move onto the ark."

"Yes," said Noah, "and I am pleased to see Ham working so hard without a word of complaint. He actually seems to enjoy the work. Remember, many years ago, how I worried and prayed for him. Now he is responsible and hard-working. I thank God that he has changed and wants to live in God's will, although I fear he still struggles greatly to follow the Lord God. Sometimes he doesn't think of the consequences of his actions and how it will affect others. Were it not for the love of his dear wife, Lea, and the patience of everyone in the family, I don't know where he would be today. Yet, in his heart I know Ham loves God and wants to do the right thing.

"The evil around us has made it even harder for Ham and everyone. I have seen the rise of wickedness beyond anything I could have imagined. I have tried so hard for so many years to warn everyone, yet no one has listened and repented. The people rejoice in evil.

"The evil one seems to have increasing control of their lives. He has used the priests to lead the people further and further away from God. And now it appears their hearts have become so hard they think only of evil—continually!

"God will send the animals soon. The ark is almost ready and I know the time for repentance is all but over."

Shem looked down at the furniture that had been carried from the house. He realized how short the time really was. Life as they had always known it was going to change forever. Yet it was important that they bring all that they would need from the old world to the new one that was to come.

The trees and plants had been prepared for transport on the ark. These would be their orchards and gardens in the new world. Food for the family had been stored near the living quarters on the top level. Feed for the animals was to be kept near the stalls on the two lower decks. Workmen, for days, had taken loads of straw into the ark as bedding for the animals.

The Animals Arrive

Since early morning everyone in Noah's family had been amazed at the hundreds of birds that had come to the ark. They circled in the sky and then flew into the huge vessel. Many went straight to the cages prepared for them—directed by the hand of God, thought Noah. There were exactly seven each of the different fowls of the air everyone observed. His family was in awe of what was happening before their eyes.

Rebecca had just stepped to the door of the ark with Noah, when suddenly out of the trees walked two dragons with three horns to their heads. Then from the other side of the clearing two large tigers strolled. Very quickly there seemed to be animals coming from all directions—giraffes, bears, gazelles, beasts of every kind and description.

Many were strange, completely unknown to them. But of each, there were both a male and female.

Noah saw two young behemoths lumbering over the hill, and he burst out laughing. God knew many adults would be too tall for the height of each floor. So He was sending mostly young ones of all the large beasts. Some animals arrived by sevens—three pairs of male and female, and an additional male.

Ham and Japheth brought food for the animals. They would need a big meal before going aboard the ark to await the Flood. As soon as the beasts

had their fill, they entered the ark and Noah and Shem led them to their stalls. Their wives came running to help with the animals. It was quiet, cool, and dark in the interior of the ark. The animals quickly settled down.

News of the arrival of thousands of beasts at the ark spread quickly. Curious people came running from the city below, questioning one another. "Why are the creatures behaving in such a strange manner? Could Noah have been right after all? Were the temple priests wrong, as he had said?"

The temple priests arrived. Seeing that their authority was being undermined, they were enraged. The priests moved among the crowd spreading lies. "We told you not to listen to Noah. This is proof of what he really is—a sorcerer! This is unnatural. He has bewitched the animals. Don't go near the ark or he will cast a spell on you."

Noah called out to people to turn to God and join him on the ark, but the crowd drew back. They *chose* to listen to lies rather than God's truth.

God Shuts the Door

The priests of the city stood together some distance from the ark and watched with smug satisfaction. "Noah will soon learn his lesson," the chief priest gloated. "Finally, that troublemaker has preached his last sermon. He will never have an opportunity to challenge our authority again. Noah and his family are trapped in the ark, and there will be no escape! He has helped seal his own fate by coating the ark with pitch. It will make a fire so hot there will be nothing left but fine ashes."

The priests had known if they just waited a few days, the people would get over their amazement of the animals arriving at the ark. The priests used the event to turn the people against Noah. In the temples and on the street corners, they cried out that Noah was an evil wizard whose enchantments would bring destruction to them all if they were not rid of him.

The priests had gathered townspeople together in front of the new temple and had worked the mob up into a frenzy. "Burn Noah," they said, "and you can divide all his lands and wealth among yourselves." The priests and a lone giant passed out unlit torches and led the mob through the streets and out of town toward the ark.

Even the men who had worked for Noah and had always received fair treatment and good wages from him were among the mob. They didn't agree with all that was being said, but they had been swept along with the emotions of the others.

Jabez and Huldah stood on the sidelines watching. Their precious daughter was on that ark. They had tried to talk her out of this craziness. Now the mob wanted to burn the ark and kill everyone in it. Even in her fear for Lea, Huldah was glad she had convinced Jabez not to board the ark with Noah's family.

The priests passed a burning lamp among the mob, lighting torches for the attack on the ark. It had been so easy. They understood greed and how to manipulate the masses. They would get others to do the dirty work, but they alone would reap the profits. The priests had already planned how they would divide up Noah's wealth among themselves.

Noah and Rebecca stood in the door of the ark and watched the mob on the hill. Noah said, "I see the giant standing with the priests is the same one who wanted to buy our Sarene. He has waited a long time to get his revenge."

Shem and Ham walked up behind their parents to tell them the last of the animals had been settled down in their stalls. It had been a week of hard work getting all the animals placed. Everyone had felt the need to hurry. Each one labored night and day to care for and place the animals. Japheth, Sarene, and Rachel were nearly finished feeding the birds on the top deck and would soon join them at the door to keep an eye on the mob.

Lea, walking toward the door, had the strangest feeling she was being followed. She turned around and began to laugh. The llamas had broken free from their stall and were following her hoping for an extra snack. She heard a loud noise and turned to look out the door. The smile on her face turned to a look of horror.

From inside the ark they saw the mob racing down the hill to attack them. Torches waving in the air clearly defined their intent.

Shem and Ham turned and ran to close the door with the pulley system. Before they could reach the pulleys the door closed by itself!

In the ark there was a sudden silence. With the door closed the screaming of the mob could no longer be heard. No one moved as each tried to absorb what had happened.

Noah put his arm around Rebecca and softly spoke to his family, "It was the hand of the Lord God that closed the door. We have done all that He instructed us to do. He patiently waited for many years for mankind to repent and turn from his evil ways. Instead of listening to the words of God everyone mocked Him and laughed. Now He has closed the final barrier between righteousness and sin. There is no more we can do, the rest is in the hands of God."

The Wrath of God

The men running at the front of the mob were only a short distance from the ramp leading into the ark when it had swung upward on strong hinges. It slammed shut with a deep resounding thud, completely blocking the entrance. God himself had shut Noah and his family in, sealed from any harm. They were in the will of God and under His protection.

Balancing themselves on the scaffold that had supported the ramp, a few men tried to pry at the edges of the door with their fingers. But they quickly realized their efforts were useless and joined the rest of the mob gathering scrap wood and brush. This they placed in piles at the base of the ark to start fires.

Suddenly, the ground began to violently heave and roll. Everyone was thrown to the ground, only to fall again in the struggle to stand. A rumbling noise under their feet grew louder and louder until it drowned out everything else. The ground began to split open and great cracks ripped across the land. The place where the priests had been standing was now a gaping hole. The earth had swallowed them!

As some cracks grew deeper and wider, fountains of fire began to shoot straight up into the air. Huge plumes of smoke and ash rose and blobs of molten rock landed all around the terrified crowd. From other cracks farther away water could be seen hurtling skyward. The force of the water quickly widened the cracks until enormous rivers were gushing from them.

32

Then a violent wind seemed to come from no-where. The trees began to bend and break. Tree branches flying through the air struck several people. The torches the townspeople had lit in anger fell to the ground, forgotten. They no longer cared about Noah and his ark. Turning from the ark, the stricken men and women sought to seek safety in their homes. Horrified, they looked down on a ruin that had been the town. Some buildings were completely gone. Nothing was left but piles of rubble. Buildings that still stood were badly damaged.

Next came the thing that most struck fear in their hearts. A few drops of water began to fall on them from the sky. Gently at first, but soon it became a deluge. Never before had water come down from the sky. Rain! No, it couldn't be. Noah had been right all along!

Panic in the Streets

The mob turned from the ark and ran toward the town where the buildings continued to crumble from the constant quaking of the earth. Men and women raced down the hills to the coast, slipping and falling as the rain seemed to pour down even harder. They were frantic to get to their homes and save treasured belongings. *Then we can escape to the high ground above the ocean,* they thought.

A tall man in a green robe shoved an old woman out of his way. His fear and greed drove him to reach the city before the others. He had seen the priests fall into the depths of the earth. The man knew where the priests kept the temple tax money and that they would never return for it. As he ran, his heavy gold necklace kept pounding against his chest. *This might not turn out so bad,* he thought. If he could get the money from the temple and find shelter in the mountains, he would be a rich man when this was over.

The rain and thunder was so loud it was hard to think. As the fountains of the deep poured forth from the earth and the rain beat down from above, streets in the lower parts of the city began to flood. The rushing currents knocked grown men off their feet. Everything seemed to be happening at once. Rubble from collapsing buildings had blocked some doorways, and people were lowering valuables and supplies from upper stories as they prepared to flee from their homes. A woman screamed for help from a second-story window. A thief was stealing money from her mother in the street below. But no one listened to her or cared.

There were some people who remembered the things Noah had said. Why hadn't they

34

listened when they had the chance, they asked themselves. Now it was too late! Other people cursed God or blamed Noah for the terrible things that were happening. Some planned to return to the ark, force open the door, and throw Noah and his family out and take their places.

No one realized that far out at sea a giant wall of water, higher than the new temple had been, was racing toward the city. There would be no escape from God's judgment.

35

Safe in the Ark

As the family sat around the table in the living area, they were in a somber mood. For days the ground beneath the ark had quaked and rumbled. The sound of the pounding rain on the ark was as loud as a herd of stampeding horses. Strange booming noises were heard from time to time. The men attempted to see what was causing them, but the rain was coming down so hard they could barely see past the edge of the ark when they opened a shutter. To keep out the fierce wind and rain, all of the shutters along the bank of windows at the top of the ark had been closed.

The temperature had dropped so that it was necessary to keep a fire in the baking oven which kept the living and sleeping area somewhat warm. Except for the hanging lamps and the light from the baking oven, the inside of the ark was dark as night.

Safe inside the thick walls of the ark, most of the animals had gone into a strange, deep sleep when the earthquakes had begun. Noah was worried, at first, that the animals might be ill or dying. He had never seen them behave in this manner before. However, when he bent close to them he could hear the sound of faint breathing. They were in a deep, peaceful sleep.

The family had gathered in the living area, finding strength in each other's presence. Together they prayed and asked for God's guidance and protection.

Lea grieved for her lost parents and turned to Ham for comfort. "If only they had listened to your father and turned to God they could be here with us," she said as she wept onto his shoulder.

Noah, hearing his daughter-in-law, stood and said, "Lea, you know your father, Jabez, was more than my employee, he was my friend. When I put him in charge of the work crews building the ark, I prayed he and your mother would put their trust in God. I had hoped that when the time came they would be on board the ark he helped build.

"I am so sorry, my dear, I wish things were different. At one time I thought your father believed. I think he was almost persuaded." Noah sadly shook his head.

Just at that moment the ark suddenly moved. Then another movement. A shifting motion, and then they were floating. The two dogs with them in the living area began pacing. The pair of cats ran beneath the table and crouched low to the floor.

Noah and his family quickly looked at each other. It had finally happened. The flood waters had reached the great meadow, once high above the sea. The city, their home, and all that was familiar was gone.

Rebecca hurried to the baking oven to see if the pot of soup cooking there was in danger of tipping over, but it was safe. Sarene found

the broom and swept burning embers back
from the front edge of the oven.

Noah looked up to see the oil lamps swinging, but
he could tell they were secure. He looked about
and everything seemed to be safe. "Quickly, sons,
go below and see to the animals," he said.

Shem, Ham, and Japheth hurriedly lit small lamps
to light their way through the darkness to the
animals. Looking in the stalls and cages, Noah's
sons found them all fast asleep.

In a short time they returned to the living
quarters and reported that all was well.

And the flood was forty days upon the earth; and the waters increased, and bare up the ark, and it was lift up above the earth. And the waters prevailed exceedingly upon the earth; and all the high hills, that were under the whole heaven, were covered.

Genesis 7:17-19

Daily Activities

The first few months on the ark were worse than anyone had expected. The flood waters were not only caused by pounding rain, but by the bursting open of the fountains of the great deep. Vast underground seas were freed to surge upward. Beneath the ark, the crust of the earth was breaking apart and shifting.

Great waves and violent winds pushed the ark into a constant rolling and pitching motion. Noah's family had never experienced anything like this before. They had been on ships before, but had never dealt with high waves and seasickness. They ate very little at first, and only food that needed no preparation.

The few times Noah had climbed to the catwalk along the top of the ark to look outside he saw nothing but water along the vast horizon. He would stare at the world before him, grief clutching his heart—they were truly alone in all the world.

Finally, the movement of the ark settled down so that those inside could begin, as much as possible, a normal life. The motion was far from calm, but did permit some activities to be done. It was much easier for them to keep their balance, and in time they had adjusted more and more to the movements of the ark.

Noah had been keeping track of the days since the day the Lord God had shut them in. Every night before he and Rebecca went to sleep, he cut a small notch in the beam next to their bed. On every seventh day he cut a deeper notch to mark off the weeks.

Over the years Rebecca had lovingly trained her daughters-in-law in the skills they would need to know in the new world. Before the Flood they had been doing more and more to become self-sufficient and less dependent on others.

Rebecca took great pleasure in preparing delicious meals for her family. Now the kitchen area was always filled with the aroma of baking breads and pastries.

The women had grown close, and Rebecca was loved as if she were their very own mother. In the living area they worked well together. Each one was pleased that she could spend her time being productive.

Sarene and Lea enjoyed working together spinning wool and weaving clothing and blankets for the family. They teased one another and often called out to Rachel to rescue one of Sarene's balls of yarn from the playful cat.

Rachel's love of animals found her, as often as possible, engaged in their feeding and care. She

often accompanied the men as they went below to care for the larger animals who woke up every few days for food and water.

The women enjoyed the sounds of the birds that were housed near the living area. Most of the birds were kept in cages, but some of the small ones, like the hummingbirds, were free to fly where they wished in the cavernous interior of the ark.

The antics of the hummingbirds often kept the family entertained. Rachel would prepare a sweet nectar to feed them and they would dart around her like bees around a flower. She would laugh when the tiny female tried to pull out one of her hairs for nesting material.

Planning Ahead

Noah sat up on the edge of his bed. He stretched, yawned, and rubbed the sleep from his eyes. He looked over at his marks in the beam and counted them. It had been 150 days since the flood had begun.

One day had become much like any other. He and his sons spent most of their time caring for the animals. He remembered how he had worried about their ability to feed the thousands of animals God would send. He should have trusted God more.

God had caused the animals to fall into a deep sleep. Each day, some of them would wake up needing food and attention. But there were never more animals awake at any one time than he and his sons could care for.

Noah could hear Rebecca preparing breakfast in the cooking area. He quickly dressed and joined the others who had gathered at the dining table.

Noah took his place at the table and led his family in prayer. "Lord God, Creator of heaven and earth and all that is in them, we thank You for Your loving care. Today we have been aboard the ark a little over five months. You have brought us safely through the terrible storms. Sometimes we feared the ark would sink. Please forgive our doubting. We know that You are faithful to Your word. We thank You now for this meal and ask You to bless us this day."

After breakfast Noah, Shem, Japheth, and Ham left the women and went below to see which animals were awake today. The elephants saw them and began trumpeting. And some other animals nearby were roused from their sleep.

"Feed the elephants first," laughed Noah. "We don't want them waking every creature on the ark." He turned and saw the koalas scurrying toward him. They had seen the eucalyptus branches in his hand. A koala hugged him on each leg.

"This won't do," Noah said, looking down at the fuzzy pair, "I can't walk." He picked one up and placed it over his shoulder, and led its mate to a nearby bench.

"We have some especially hearty appetites this morning," Ham said as he lifted another large forkful of hay up to the mouth of a great beast with an ax-shaped headcrest.

The okapi in the next stall strained its neck to reach the forkful of hay as it went by. Ham reached out and gave it a pat. "Your turn is coming," he said. "I'll feed you and your beautiful mate next."

Finally, every hungry mouth and beak had been fed. The four men cleaned the stalls of the animals they had just fed and spread fresh straw for bedding. When the animals had been watered the men sat down to rest and talk.

Suddenly they were thrown off balance! The ark had struck something. Shem fell off his bench in an undignified heap, and Japheth, who had been leaning against an upright beam fell to the floor. He rolled across the deck and under the stall door of the stately giraffes.

Sprawled on his back, Japheth looked up to find himself face to face with a startled giraffe. Japheth burst into laughter at the surprised expression on the creature's face—wide-eyed, it blinked its long lashes. The giraffe very gently and carefully spread his four legs to avoid stepping on Japheth as he crawled out from under him.

"We've landed on solid ground," said Shem. The four men looked at each other and without a word spoken rushed to the catwalk.

It Will Soon Be Over

Noah and his sons were breathless when they reached the catwalk. Rebecca and the other women joined them at the top of the ark a moment later. They immediately began throwing open the window shutters.

They knew the ark had run aground on the top of a mountain, for all they could see was water. They felt joyful, however, to know that the flood waters were going down.

Many days went by and still they could not see land. The ark was no longer floating, yet they still felt movement below them. There were earthquakes as the land shifted and rumbled. New

mountains were being formed, rising up as the flood waters receded.

One morning after breakfast Japheth went to the catwalk alone. Suddenly the others heard his shout, "Land! I see land!" Everyone rushed to join him at the row of windows. "Look, there in the distance—a mountaintop," he cried as he pointed to the horizon.

Rachel and Lea grabbed each other and laughed and cried at the same time, jumping up and down like children.

Noah turned to Rebecca and smiled, "We have waited 74 days since the ark came to rest on this

mountain to see other land. The winds that God has sent will help dry the land so the grasses and trees will grow once again."

The next 40 days brought rapid changes as more and more land came into view. Noah was encouraged and released a raven and a dove. The dove returned but the raven was not seen again. Noah knew there was no suitable place for the dove to land and find food. The raven, a scavenger, could survive on any dead animals it might find.

Seven days later, Noah sent out the dove again. The family, having waited for hours, had all but given up hope for her return. Then Rachel cried out, "Here comes the dove, over to the left. You

can barely see her." As the dove got closer, they could tell she had something in her beak.

The dove circled the ark to get her bearings before sweeping down to the open windows. She saw Noah's outstretched hand and landed on it, "It's an olive leaf," exclaimed Noah. "Things are beginning to grow again on the earth!"

Noah's family longed to leave the ark and walk upon the earth. But, another three months went by—time for the land to dry and plants to grow that would feed the animals. Finally, 371 days after the flood began, God told Noah and his family they could leave the ark. The next part of their adventure would soon begin.

Leaving the Ark

The door of the ark lowered slowly. It creaked and groaned as Japheth and Ham turned the pulley handles. It had been closed for over a year and was still swollen from the waters of the flood.

Noah had been concerned that the door of the ark would be too high up to use as an exit ramp. But God had placed the ark in a perfect spot—a depression in the ground at the top of the mountain. When the door was lowered it rested on a gentle slope.

Noah and his family stood in the doorway and looked out at the landscape before them. Even though the men had cut a hole in the roof of the ark and walked out to see how dry the land was, nothing could have prepared them for the starkness that lay before them.

Rebecca had hoped she would recognize the landscape. A place near their old home. But nothing was familiar.

Noah shook his head. "God has changed the surface of the earth so much that nothing remains the same. Not only has His judgment been on all life on the land, but upon the earth itself.

"I know it looks barren, but there are already plants and young trees on the hillsides beginning to grow. We have seeds, vines, and young trees to plant for our immediate needs. God has provided all that we will need in this new world. He will bless us as we continue to obey Him."

The family suddenly became aware of a growing chorus of roars, grunts, and screeches. The bright light coming in the open door had made the animals eager to be free.

"Come on everyone, there's work to be done," said Shem as he turned back into the ark. "Let us feed the animals one last time."

Ham had to jump to the side as the ostriches raced past him. The anteaters hesitated at the door and blinked their eyes.

The burly bears lumbered by, glad to stretch their legs. They wrestled and rolled on the ground like cubs. Above them thousands of birds and other winged creatures took to the air. They dipped and soared in the air currents, joyously flapping wings long unused for flight.

Noah turned with alarm when he heard the ramp creaking under the weight of the pair of behemoths. He was afraid the wood might splinter and injure one of them—but the strong ramp held fast. When these long-necked giants had come aboard, they were no larger than elephants. Now they even towered over the giraffes.

Some animals stayed around the ark for days, reluctant to leave at first. But soon most of them wandered away and did not return.

The animals that the family would need for survival and for sacrifice were kept in their stalls and cages.

Worshiping at God's Altar

Noah and his sons struggled up a rocky trail to the ark from the slope below. The mountain was steeper at the top and climbing was more difficult. That morning they had gathered stones and built an altar further down the mountain.

When they reached the ark, the women had the noon meal waiting for them. After they had eaten, Noah said, "We must gather together those birds and beasts that are to be sacrificed. Let us go and select one each of the animals God sent by sevens."

"One of each, Father?" Ham asked. "Of the tame animals that we will need to start life over again? Aren't those animals some of the most valuable of all to us?"

"Yes, Ham," Noah replied patiently. "And I want us to choose the most perfect ones. God has brought us safely through the most terrible time the world has ever seen. He deserves the best we have."

Noah's family descended the rocky mountain slowly, to take the animals along the smoothest way. Everyone helped carry the birds in cages. When they reached the altar, the men tethered the four-legged beasts, tying their legs with ropes to keep them from wandering away.

Then Noah called everyone around him. It was time to thank and praise God for their deliverance. Noah selected a ram as the first beast to sacrifice. The sheep was a perfect creature without blemish. Then Noah led his family in prayer.

"Lord God, great Creator of heaven and earth, we come to You with humble hearts. You delivered us from a sin-filled world, yet we are still sinners through our ancestors Adam and Eve. When they sinned, You taught them that there could be no forgiveness of sin without the shedding of blood. You, yourself, first slew animals to shed their innocent blood in a sacrificial act. Then You covered Adam and Eve in their skins. Thus, You showed mankind that an atonement, or covering for sin, must be a blood sacrifice."

Noah then placed the ram on the altar and made an offering of it to God. "This we have learned to do from You, Lord God, through our ancestors in the Garden of Eden," continued Noah. "May none of us ever be as Cain, seeking forgiveness through offerings of our own efforts—false proof of our own works and worthiness, for we are most unworthy."

After the other animals were sacrificed, Noah praised God for His grace and protection to his family. He listed all of the good things God had done for them and asked His blessing on their lives in the new world.

When Shem felt a cooling breeze, he was the first to look up. What he saw took his breath away. A light rain fell over the mountaintop in the distance, and curving across the sky was an arch of many colors. Shem had never seen anything so wondrous before. The colors seemed to glow and he could see through them. Speechless, he pointed to the sky. In silence they all stared at this marvel—the first rainbow!

Building a New Life

The sweet fragrance of the incense from the burnt offering on the altar drifted upward and filled the air. The blood sacrifice and Noah's humble prayer of thanksgiving for deliverance from the sinful world and the preservation of his family through the Flood was pleasing to God. And in His great love, God brought comfort to the eight men and women who faced building a new life in this strange new world.

In spite of mankind's sinful nature, God promised that never again would He judge the earth. Nor would He again destroy everything living as long as the earth continued in its present form.

This was a great blessing for Noah's family to know. For a few days later, when they were first caught in a heavy rainfall on the mountainside, Lea and Rachel clung to each other in terror. Noah gathered the family around himself to remind them of God's promise. Noah assured them that although there would now be rains, and sometimes floods; never again would a worldwide flood destroy all life on the land. After that, none of them were fearful again when it rained. In time, they all grew to fully realize that the falling rains were but another blessing from God. The rains watered their crops and cleansed the earth. In fact, they would all look up when it rained, hoping to see another bright bow—a token of God's covenant, His promise to all mankind.

Noah and his family stayed in the ark for a time, but the mountaintop soon grew very cold. So they fashioned tents to live in and moved down to the warmer valley.

There was always much to do, and the days never seemed long enough. Everyone worked from early morning till long past sundown. They were adjusting to temperature changes and the strong winds that often blew.

When snow first began to fall on the mountains, Noah and his sons salvaged some timbers from the ark. It was backbreaking work to bring them down. But they had nothing else to build with. Only small saplings grew from the earth as yet. The family used the timbers to start building a more permanent home they could share if the valley became as cold as the mountaintop.

Fortunately, as time went on, they would find that the valley remained warm most of the year; but the ark would be lost from their sight under an almost permanent blanket of ice and snow. One bright morning Noah was watering the vineyard he had planted, and stood up to rest his back for a moment. He looked at his family, all hard at work near him, and felt filled with love. Shem and Sarene's baby was expected any day. And Japheth and Ham were going to be fathers in just a month or two. Noah and Rebecca were looking forward to the day they could hold their first grandchild and to many years of hearing the laughter of children again.

Noah bent over and resumed his work in the vineyard. He thought how quickly the earth was changing. It was turning green and the young orchards they had planted were budding. Soon it would be time to think about building granaries to hold the harvest from the fields. Noah whispered a prayer of thanks to God for blessing them so abundantly in building a new life.

Teaching the Next Generation

The Flood had changed the world more than any of Noah's family had realized at first. The earth no longer had a warm, gentle climate from pole to pole. There began to be hot summers and very cold winters in some parts of the world.

God had told Noah that mankind could now depend upon fixed times of the year to plant seeds and harvest the resulting crops. The regularity of the seasons, the heat and the cold—just as day followed night—would not cease. The unfailing repetition of this new cycle came to remind Noah's family that they worshiped a God of order.

Occasionally the family would talk about how strange it was to be the only people on earth. It was so quiet. Most of the animals had disappeared after leaving the ark. God had put a new fear of mankind in the beasts. Some of the wild ones fled as if in terror after God made this change in them. When Noah's family spoke of this, they wondered how far some of the animals had gone, and if they would ever see them again. Japheth had recalled a few of the great dragons with terrible teeth and claws he hoped would never wander back their way. The rest of the family had heartily agreed with him.

Other things were different in the new world. They all noticed that crops did not grow as well as they had before the Flood. The plants did not grow as tall, nor did the fruit grow as large. Noah wondered if this was because the earth itself was different. Had the flood waters washed away something in the ground, or in the air that the plants needed to grow as they once did?

When God had blessed Noah and his sons after the Flood, He had given them a new authority—to eat animals for food. Until then, they had dined only on plant food, just as all of their ancestors had done since the time of Adam and Eve. Noah and his family found the taste of meat agreeable when they got used to it.

Perhaps God wanted them to eat the flesh of animals now because He knew they could no longer get all the nutrition their bodies needed from plants grown in the flood-washed earth.

God had commanded Noah's sons and their wives to have many children and repopulate the earth. And as time passed, their families did increase.

The family decided that Ham, who truly had worked harder on the new brick structure than anyone else—and who soon had the most children—should live in it.But, in fact, the others preferred to live in tents after their long confinement on the ark.

On a day that Noah and Rebecca walked together to visit Shem and Sarene, the world could not

have been a nicer place. They found
Shem and his family in their garden, seated
under a shade tree. Shem was teaching his children about God, the old world, and God's prom-
ises to them in the new world. Noah thought of
the days long gone when he had sat under a tree
and spoke of God with his own dear children.

There was peace in Noah's heart. The evil one
had tried to destroy the sons of Adam and failed
miserably. And someday, the Promised Son would
come to have complete victory over the evil one.
Until then, Noah knew that if his descendants
would only continue to teach their children to
worship and trust God, the world would always be
a wonderful place to live.

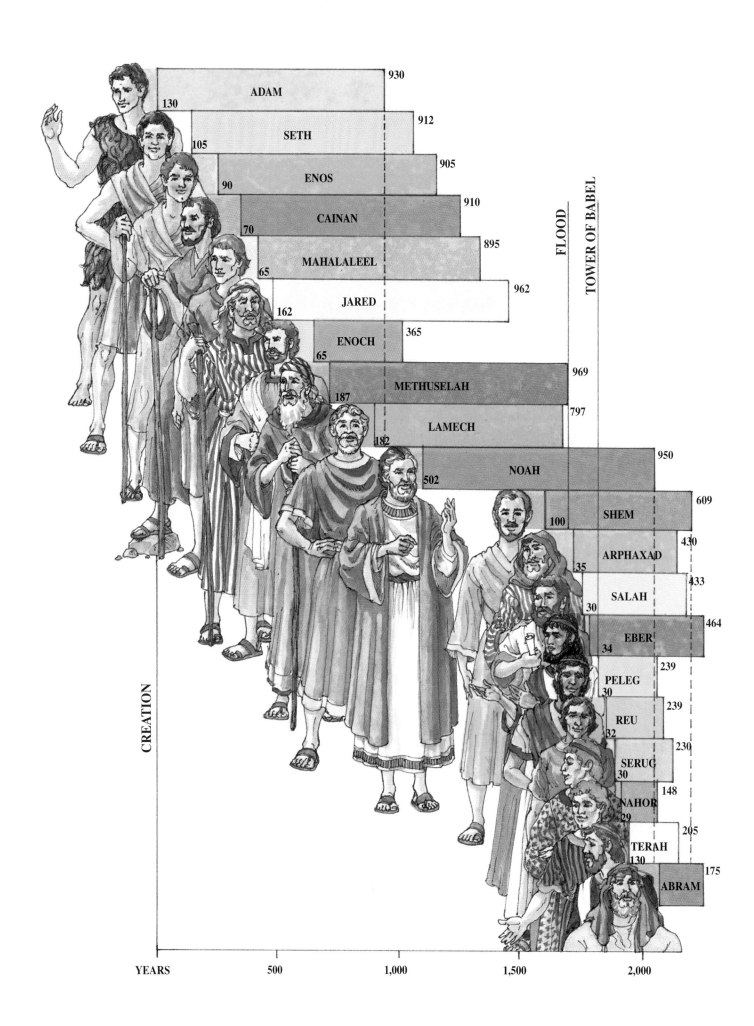

Part II
The Family of Adam

Everyone alive today, or who has ever lived, is a descendant of Adam. We are all related, even though most of us are very, very distant cousins.

Even though different groups of people are called races (Caucasian, Hispanic, etc.) there is only one race—the human race.

Looking at the illustration of the genealogy of Adam to Abram (Abraham) you may be surprised to see that Adam was still alive when Noah's father, Lamech, was born. Or that Noah and Shem were probably at the Tower of Babel when God confused the languages.

It is very easy to "lump" Genesis 1-11 into four parts:

- Creation
- Adam and Eve in the Garden of Eden
- Noah and the Flood
- The Tower of Babel

But, as you can see, lives overlapped, sometimes by hundreds of years. The men represented here are the first 20 generations in the earthly family of Jesus Christ. Each of them lived full lives before the Lord God. They raised their children to honor and love God. Each one took his responsibility before the Lord seriously. They must have led very interesting lives with changes taking place constantly. Unfortunately, the Bible doesn't give us a lot of details about their daily lives.

For example, the Bible says that Methuselah's father, Enoch, "walked with God: and he was not; for God took him" (Gen. 5:24). I don't know about you, but I would like to know a lot more about what happened and how God "took him." The world must have already been full of violence and evil for "walking with God" to be so unusual.

Don't you think Methuselah told his family all about Enoch? With no television to distract them, families did a lot more talking and told many stories about their family history.

Shem may even have known Abraham when he was a young boy. Perhaps Abraham was raised

hearing firsthand accounts of the Flood and what it was like to watch the animals walk out of a lush forest and into the Ark. And then a year later watch those same animals exit into a nearly barren world. How different everything was. There were no cities or forests. It would have been especially strange to know that they were the *only* people alive on all the earth.

The world before the Flood was a *very* different place! One of the biggest differences is the length of people's lives. The longest age *recorded* was Methuselah who lived 969 years and died the same year as God brought the Flood.

How could anyone live to be hundreds of years old? No one knows for sure, but there are several possibilities. Before the Flood there may have been a vapor canopy to keep out the harmful ultraviolet rays. It's also possible there were plants that slowed aging or even something in the air, water, or soil that is now buried in the depth of today's oceans. Even today modern scientists have been unable to discover what causes aging. They can describe it and watch it happen, but they're not sure *why* it happens.

Because their lives were so much longer they would have "aged" differently. With today's much shorter life spans we think of someone over 80 as *very* old. But if you lived to be several hundred years old, 80 would be very young. We don't know if people reached adulthood at the same rate before the Flood. Perhaps their childhood lasted 20 to 30 years. Whatever it was, the aging process was normal for that time and would not have seemed strange. Noah was already 500 years old before his sons Shem, Ham, and Japheth were born, and lived hundreds of years after the Flood.

Things changed immediately after the Flood. Arphaxad, born after the Flood, lived 430 years. Eight generations later Abraham lived only 175 years. Soon 70 years was the normal life span.

God gave the first generations long lives to worship Him, but many of Adam's family used those long lives to turn away from Him.

The Family of Noah

The descendants of Noah listed in Genesis 10 (next page) are believed to be the language groups that migrated away from Babel (Gen. 10:32). Some of the names in Genesis 10 are hard to identify, and some seemed to have died out. Many different ideas have been proposed, but as close as we can tell they became the nations below.

Shem

Primary responsibility: maintaining man's spiritual life.

Significant achievements: Theology—Developed great religious systems—both true and false.

Tribes & Nations: middle-east

Arabia, Arabs, Aramaeans, Assyrians, Hebrews, Lydians (Asia Minor), Persians, Syrians, Yemen.

Ham

Primary responsibility: man's physical survival and dominion over the earth.

Significant achievements: Technology—Builders, inventors, navigators, explorers, cultivators, tradesmen, and warriors.

Tribes & Nations: south & east

Africa, Arabia, Assyria, Babylonia, Canaanites, China, Crete, Egypt, Ethiopia, Hittites, Japan, Libya, Mongol nations, Phoenicia, North & South American Indians, Sabeans, South Sea Islanders, Sudan, Sumeria.

Japheth

Primary responsibility: developing philosophical systems and scientific methods.

Significant achievements: Science & Philosophy— Philosophers, scientists, explorers, and colonizers.

Tribes & Nations: north & west

Armenia, Aryans, Cyprus, Denmark, Europeans, Georgia, Germany, Greece, Italy, Macedonia, North Africa, Northern India, Rhodes, Russia, Saxon, Scandia, Scythians, Spain, Turkey, Wales.

God that made the world and all things therein. . . . hath made of one blood all nations of men for to dwell on all the face of the earth, and hath determined the times before appointed, and the bounds of their habitation (Acts 17:24-26).

The table above is based on Genesis 10; *Noah's Three Sons* by Arthur C. Custance (Grand Rapids, MI: Zondervan Publishing House, 1975), p. 26-118; *The Genesis Record* by Henry Morris (Grand Rapids, MI: Baker Book House, 1979), p. 239-263; and study notes in *The Defender's Study Bible* with annotations by Henry M. Morris (Grand Rapids, MI: World Publishing, 1995), p. 28-30.

Questions and Answers

Q. *Who wrote Genesis 10?*

A. Most scholars believe Shem kept track of the three families. He seems to have lost touch with the "Hamites" and the "Japhethites" after the confusion of languages at the Tower of Babel.

Q. *Why does the same country appear in more than one genealogy?*

A. Modern country borders do not always match original national boundaries. For example, the study of languages (linguistics) shows the evidence of two major tribal groups in Arabia.

Q. *The Bible always lists Noah's sons in the same order—Shem, Ham, and Japheth. Why did you make Ham the youngest?*

A. Noah's sons are not listed in the order of their birth. Genesis 10:21 says that Shem is "the brother of Japheth the elder," which seems to say Japheth is the oldest, although, other scholars feel it would be more correct to translate it as, "the elder brother of Japheth."

Genesis 9:24 calls Ham the "younger son" of Noah which seems to indicate that he is the youngest of the three.

In the biblical genealogies the names of the children are not always listed in the order of their birth. The male child that would be the spiritual leader of his family or tribe is many times listed first.

Shem may be mentioned first because he is the ancestor of Abraham and therefore, in the line of the coming Messiah, Jesus Christ.

Noah may have had other sons and daughters, but they did not follow the Lord God and died in the Flood. All we do know is that Noah was 500 before he had Shem, Ham, or Japheth.

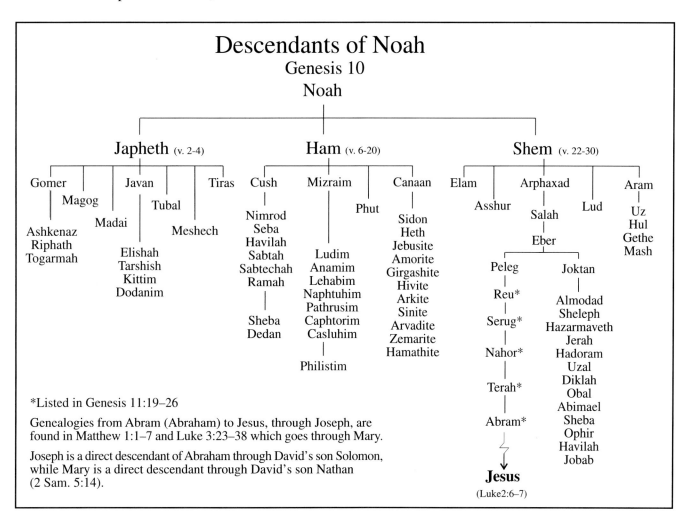

Descendants of Noah
Genesis 10
Noah

Japheth (v. 2-4)

Gomer — Ashkenaz, Riphath, Togarmah
Magog
Madai
Javan — Elishah, Tarshish, Kittim, Dodanim
Tubal
Meshech
Tiras

Ham (v. 6-20)

Cush — Nimrod, Seba, Havilah, Sabtah, Sabtechah, Ramah — Sheba, Dedan
Mizraim — Ludim, Anamim, Lehabim, Naphtuhim, Pathrusim, Caphtorim, Casluhim — Philistim
Phut
Canaan — Sidon, Heth, Jebusite, Amorite, Girgashite, Hivite, Arkite, Sinite, Arvadite, Zemarite, Hamathite

Shem (v. 22-30)

Elam
Asshur
Arphaxad — Salah — Eber — Peleg — Reu* — Serug* — Nahor* — Terah* — Abram* ⟿ **Jesus** (Luke 2:6–7)
Eber — Joktan — Almodad, Sheleph, Hazarmaveth, Jerah, Hadoram, Uzal, Diklah, Obal, Abimael, Sheba, Ophir, Havilah, Jobab
Lud
Aram — Uz, Hul, Gethe, Mash

*Listed in Genesis 11:19–26

Genealogies from Abram (Abraham) to Jesus, through Joseph, are found in Matthew 1:1–7 and Luke 3:23–38 which goes through Mary.

Joseph is a direct descendant of Abraham through David's son Solomon, while Mary is a direct descendant through David's son Nathan (2 Sam. 5:14).

— 7 days —	— 40 days —	—————— 110 days ——————	—— 74 days ——

God Shuts the Door

Noah and the animals entered the ark. The time for judgment had come. "The Lord shut him in" (Gen. 7:16) tells of God's love and protection for those who trust in Him.

Flood Begins

"All the fountains of the great deep broken up, and the windows of heaven were opened. And the rain was upon the earth forty days and forty nights" (Gen. 7:11-12).

The Flood Covers the Whole Earth

"The waters prevailed exceedingly upon the earth; and all the high hills, that were under the whole heaven, were covered. Fifteen cubits upward did the waters prevail; and the mountains were covered" (Gen. 7:19-20).

All of the land was under water, enormous earthquakes and undersea eruptions were continuing. During this time, great amounts of sedimentation occurred. The layers of mud containing "dead things" became the fossil and coal beds we have today.

15 cubits is 22.5 feet (6.75 meters)

The Ark "Lands"

"God made a wind to pass over the earth, and the waters assuaged. And the ark rested . . . upon the mountains of Ararat" (Gen. 8:1-4).

The land continues to rise as mountains and valleys form. The waters are draining into ocean basins.

It would still be months before Noah's family would set foot on dry land.

Q. *Why do you illustrate the ark with square ends instead of looking like a normal ship?*

A. The main purpose of the ark was to float. It didn't have to "go" anywhere. God would direct the winds and currents to take the ark to the resting place He had picked out. Also, with squared-off ends, the ark could hold a lot more cargo and be built on the ground. An ark with rounded ends would have required a cradle and been much more difficult to build.

Q. *How large was the ark, and what is a cubit?*

A. In Genesis 6:15 God commands Noah to build the ark and gives him the dimensions in cubits. A cubit was the distance from the tip of a man's fingers to his elbow, *approximately* 18 inches (0.45 meters). The size of the ark was to be 300 cubits (450 feet; 135 meters) long, 50 cubits (75 feet; 23 meters) wide, and 30 cubits (45 feet; 13 meters) high. It had three stories, with each of the three stories being about 15 feet (4.5 meters) high. There was a window which was one cubit (18 inches; 0.45 meters) high.

Q. *What were "gopher wood" and "pitch"?*

A. We don't know the species of tree, but it would probably have been a hard, dense wood. Pitch was a sealer for the wood. Though we don't know exactly what it was, it wasn't the coal-based product we have today. It may have been resin from trees.

Q. *Where is the ark today?*

A. Genesis 8:4 says, "The ark rested . . . upon the mountains of Ararat." In the country of Turkey are the twin mountains called Greater and Lesser Mount Ararat. There have been "eye-witness" sightings of the ark going back hundreds of years. It seems like it would be an easy job to just go find it, but the reality is far from easy.

Mount Ararat is a climber's nightmare, and some years the glaciers cover all the areas where the ark might possibly be. To top that off, the Turkish government seldom issues permits to climb the mountain. If it's there, it must not be God's time for it to be discovered.

— 40 days —	— 28 days —	— 22 days —	— 57 days —	
Mountain Tops Seen	**Noah Sends Raven**	**Dove Doesn't Return**	**The Ground Is Dry**	**New World**

Mountain Tops Seen

"The waters decreased continually until . . . were the tops of the mountains seen" (Gen. 8:5).

While the land was drying, grasses, trees, and other food sources for the animals needed time to grow.

Noah Sends Raven

"He sent forth a raven" (Gen. 8:7).

After each of four seven-day periods, Noah sends out a dove (Gen. 8:8, 10, 12).

The water level keeps dropping, and Noah wants to know if plant life is beginning to grow.

Dove Doesn't Return

"The dove; which returned not again unto him any more" (Gen. 8:12).

The little dove found she could survive outside the ark and didn't return.

The Ground Is Dry

"The earth dried" (Gen. 8:14).

It was nearly time to enter the new world. The conditions were almost ready.

"And God spake unto Noah, saying, Go forth of the ark, thou, and thy wife, and thy sons, and thy son's wives with thee" (Gen. 8:15-16).

New World

"Noah built an altar unto the Lord" (Gen. 8:20).

"Noah thanked God and praised Him. God put a rainbow in the sky to show the covenant He made" (Gen. 9:13).

Q. *The Flood waters must have been very stormy with 40 days of heavy rain and the great winds of Genesis 8:1. Wouldn't the ark have tipped over?*

A. God knew exactly what it was going to be like during the Flood. When He gave Noah the dimensions for the ark He knew how stable it needed to be.

In 1993 The Korea Research Institute of Ships and Ocean Engineering did an extensive testing on the safety of Noah's ark in "severe environments." Results showed "the ark had a superior level of safety in high winds and waves."

Dr. Henry Morris writes in *The Genesis Record* that the ark "would be exceedingly stable, almost impossible to capsize." He continues, "Even in a sea of gigantic waves, the ark could be tilted through any angle up to just short of 90° and would immediately thereafter right itself again."[1]

Q. *How could there have been enough room in the ark for two or more of every animal in the world?*

A. Not only was the ark larger than you imagine, but there weren't nearly as many animals on the ark as you might think. Pairs of each *kind*, or basic type of land-dwelling, air-breathing animal, had to be on board the ark (Gen. 7:22). We don't know how many *kinds* were alive in Noah's day, but today there are less than 20,000 different types of animals, not counting those animals who live in the sea, or those who don't breath air. Even most insects were probably not on the ark. Their eggs and larvae could have survived on floating logs outside the ark.

All modern types could, through small changes, have come from about 5,000 *kinds* or less that God originally created. But no matter how many kinds there were, we know that the ark was big enough to hold more than 50,000 animals, with room to spare!

Flood Legends

More than 270 stories and historic records of a worldwide Flood are found all over the world. Their variations from Genesis reflect the way details may change when stories are told from one generation to another. In the absence of written records, facts have a way of changing to fit in with the culture of the storyteller.

Following are just three of the many Flood legends from around the world.

Toltec

Found in the histories of the Toltec Indians of ancient Mexico is a story of the first world that lasted 1,716 years and was destroyed by a great Flood that covered even the highest mountains. Their story tells of a few men who escaped the destruction in a "toptlipetlocali," which means a closed chest. Following the great Flood, these men began to multiply and built a very high "zacuali," or a great tower, to provide a safe place if the world were destroyed again. However, the languages became confused, so different language groups wandered to other parts of the world.

The Toltecs claim they started as a family of seven friends and their wives who spoke the same language. They crossed great waters, lived in caves, and wandered 104 years till they came to Hue Hue Tlapalan (southern Mexico). The story reports that this was 520 years after the great Flood.

India

In the Indian account of the Flood, "Noah" is known as "Satyaurata," who had three sons, the eldest of whom was named Iyapeti. The other two were called Samarma and C'harma. To the first he allotted all the regions north of the Himalayas and to Sharma he gave the country of the South. But he cursed C'harma, because when the old monarch was accidentally inebriated with strong liquor made from a fermented rice, C'harma had laughed at him.

China

Ancient Chinese writings refer to a violent catastrophe that happened to the earth. They report that the entire land was flooded. The water went up to the highest mountains and completely covered all the foothills. It left the country in desolate condition for years after.

One ancient Chinese classic called the "Hihking" tells the story of Fuhi, whom the Chinese consider to be the father of their civilization. This history records that Fuhi, his wife, three sons, and three daughters escaped a great Flood. He and his family were the only people left alive on earth. After the great Flood they repopulated the world.

An ancient temple in China has a wall painting that shows Fuhi's boat in the raging waters. Dolphins are swimming around the boat and a dove with an olive branch in its beak is flying toward it.

Q. *Why did you make Noah so rich?*

A. Noah would have needed great wealth to purchase all the supplies and hire help to build the huge ark. Even after the ark was completed, other supplies would have to be purchased. Most plants would survive the Flood and grow again, but they would need time to become food crops. Noah would need to take young fruit trees, vines, and seed for crops the family would need to survive. Noah also had to provide food for the animals during the long confinement on the ark. By the time the ark was finished no one would have been willing to help Noah. God would have given Noah and his family the resources to do His will. Relying on a hostile world would not have been an option

Q. *How did you pick names for characters in the story, Noah's wife, daughters-in-law, and others?*

A. Since the names listed for men and women that lived before the Flood still mean something in the Hebrew language, it is possible that the original language given to Adam was Hebrew. The fictitious names in our story have meanings as follows:

Rebecca, "to bind," referring to the strength of the marriage bond. It was Noah's wife who, by example, taught her daughters-in-law how to be godly wives.

Rachel, "little lamb," gentleness or innocence.

Sarene (Sarah), "the princess."

Lea, "weary" or "forsaken." This seemed appropriate since her grandson was the evil Nimrod, builder of the Tower of Babel.

Jabez, the name for Lea's father means "sorrow." It seems suitable for a man who was "almost persuaded" of God's truth, but rejected it.

Huldah, mother of Lea, means "weasel, industrious." She gladly used her daughter to gain importance.

Q. *How could anything the size of the ark have been built before modern technology?*

A. Early man (starting with Gen. 1:27) was gifted with great intelligence and in some cases life spans of nearly a thousand years. Can you imagine what a civilization of "super-brains" could accomplish during such long lives?

Modern mankind gives itself a lot of credit it doesn't deserve. Yes, we have computers, airplanes, space shuttles, etc., but this technology is possible only because of the groundwork done by others before. (Don't forget, we also have the technology to blow each other to smithereens.)

Evolutionists are firmly convinced that the human race started as pond scum and over millions of years evolved upward into the outstanding specimens we are today. That must mean we are getting smarter and smarter as we evolve. Right? Wrong!

If you follow that line of reasoning it would mean as you go back in time people were less intelligent. Archaeology does not verify that conclusion. In fact, archaeology has shown mankind has, from the beginning, built great civilizations.

Q. *Can the Bible be used as a reliable history book?*

A. The well-known and respected archaeologist W. F. Albright says, "There can be no doubt that archaeology has confirmed the substantial historicity of Old Testament tradition."[2]

Q. *Genesis 8:1 says "And God remembered Noah." How could God forget Noah?*

A. God doesn't "forget" anything! When the Old Testament says that "God remembered" it speaks of God's faithful love and His action to help the one He "remembered."

Q. *Who were the giant Nephilim?*

A. The Bible talks of a tribe of giants that lived in the days of Noah (Gen. 6:4). Many theologians believe they were the children of demon-controlled men and women. The name nephilim (NEF-ah-lem) means "fallen ones."

They were so evil that they influenced *all* of the people except Noah and his family. The very next verse (v. 5) says, "The wickedness of man was great in the earth, and that *every* imagination of the thoughts of his heart was *only evil continually*" (italics mine).

Verse 11 continues with "The earth also was corrupt before God and the earth was *filled* with violence," (italics mine). For the earth to be filled with violence there must have been quite a few people alive. By the time of the Flood, 1,656 years after God created Adam, there could have been a population in the millions. That's a lot of evil!

Q. *Would there really have been a city like the one you have shown in this story at the time of Noah?*

A. We know relatively little of the world before the Flood. The Bible gives us few details. We have taken what the Bible *does* tell us, and staying faithful to the information we do have, imagined a culture that we feel is both quite possible and believable.

With long life spans and a great deal of God-given creativity, civilization developed at an unbelievable rate. Adam's son Cain built a city (Gen. 4:17), which involves more than simply erecting a few tents. A city requires government, planning, and cooperation among its citizens. By verses 20-22 we find cattle (science of animal husbandry), the harp and organ (string and wind instruments require the basic knowledge of mathematics), and brass and iron (art of metallurgy). From the very beginning, mankind possessed a keen intelligence and the ability to work together towards a common goal. Genesis 5:1 seems to describe writing; "This is the book of the generations of Adam." This seems to indicate a written language was being used at this time.

Modern archaeologists are confirming that there was a high degree of technology associated with the earliest human settlers all over the world.

Q. *Why don't we find evidence of pre-Flood civilization?*

A. The purpose of the Flood was to annihilate (destroy *completely*) the world *and* all the land creatures not on the ark (Gen. 3:13). The buildings at that time did not require sturdy construction. The earthquakes and the turbulent action of the Flood waters would have easily destroyed any buildings.

We know from Genesis 4:22 that people living before the Flood used metal alloys (different metals melted together). Brass is copper and zinc, and iron is often alloyed with another metal for strength. Dr. John Morris has been studying an interesting bronze (copper and tin) bell and an iron pot. They were discovered embedded deep in a coal bed that evolutionists say is 200 million years old.

This brings up the interesting subject of anomalies. The dictionary defines an anomaly as a "departure from the normal or common order; difficult to classify." The bronze bell and iron pot certainly qualify as anomalies. There are *hundreds* of anomalies that don't fit in the evolutionary order. Most are just ignored since they seem to rock the "evolutionary boat."

One of the current theories to explain the high degree of technology in the early civilizations is that outer-space beings visited our planet thousands of years ago and either colonized it or gave the "natives" inventions and knowledge they would not otherwise have had. As ridiculous as this sounds, there are people who are positive this is the *only* explanation for the early civilizations.

Q. *The Bible says it rained 40 days and 40 nights. Where did all that water come from?*

A. When the "fountains of the great deep" broke open, enormous amounts of steam were released. The underground reservoirs and volcanic eruptions sent water vapor into the atmosphere where it condensed and fell as rain. Many creation scientists believe there was a water-vapor canopy around the earth before the Flood and it collapsed when the Flood began.

Q. *What could cause the "giant wall of water" mentioned on page 35?*

A. Giant waves called tsunamis (soo-na-mes) are caused by an underwater earthquake or volcanic eruption. In deep water, the swells are so long and slight that ships hardly notice them. But as tsunamis reach shallow water, they pile up into crests that can be as much as 200 feet (60 meters) high. In deep water they can travel at an average speed of more than 500 miles (790 kilometers) an hour. In 1883 over 30,000 people died on the island of Java as a tsunami caused by the eruption of Krakatoa slammed into the island.

Q. *Did many animals, such as the dinosaurs, become extinct at the time of the Flood?*

A. No. We know from the fossil record that untold millions of animals perished in the Flood. However, God had a purpose for each *kind* of animal He had created, and He provided that all the *kinds* be preserved. No *kind* of animal became extinct at the time of the Flood, for God told Noah, "And of every living thing of all flesh, two of every sort shalt thou bring into the ark, to keep them alive with thee; they shall be male and female" (Gen. 6:19).

When God sent the animals to the ark, He sent two of each *kind*.

Q. *Were there really dinosaurs aboard the ark? How could a huge Brachiosaurus even get aboard the ark?*

A. God created the land animals on day 6 (Gen. 1:24-25), and that included dinosaurs. They still roamed the earth at the time of the Flood and had multiplied greatly. The fossil record shows that there were several kind*s* of dinosaurs and often varieties within the kinds.

Many animals are quite large when full grown. And large animals have *large* appetites! Of these animals, God probably sent young or juvenile ones to Noah. Not only would they take up less room and eat less, but no doubt take the rolling and pitching of the ark better.

He didn't need to send all the *varieties* of each *kind*. He did not need to send two of each dog breed. God very likely sent two dogs, probably wolf-like creatures, to be the ancestral parents of all the dog breeds we have today.

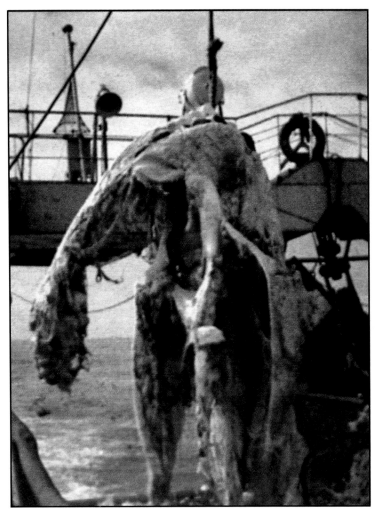

Q. *If there were dinosaurs on the ark, why aren't there any around today?*

A. When the dinosaurs left the ark after the Flood, they found a world incredibly different than the one before the Flood. Food, once abundant, would have been difficult to find. Weather that had always been pleasant would now often be hostile. Under these conditions, the dinosaurs failed to repopulate the earth and, consequently, died out.

However, dinosaurs may not be as extinct as you would think. Ever hear of the Loch Ness monster? Many people think it is a *Plesiosaur.* That's not as farfetched as you might think.

Imagine the surprise, in 1977, on board the Japanese fishing boat *Zuiyo Maru* near New Zealand, when a dead, very smelly "monster" came up in their net from a depth of over 900 feet. It is estimated the creature could have

been dead over a month. It was 32 feet long and weighed over 4,000 pounds. The fishermen measured it, photographed it, took tissue samples, and promptly threw it overboard before it could contaminate their "real catch."

The Japanese scientists who had flown in to see this wonderful "new" sea monster were a bit upset, to say the least. From all the evidence available to them, the scientists believed the creature to "look very much like a *Plesiosaur*" (PLEE-zee-uh-sawr). One scientist said, "It seems that these animals are not extinct after all. It is impossible for only one to have survived. There must be a group."[3]

Several other fishing boats were sent to the area and they all tried to net the animal. There have been several other ideas about what the creature could have been. Perhaps one day someone will catch another one, and then we'll know for sure.

Q. *What happened to the fish and air breathing animals (whales, etc.) in the sea during the Flood?*

A. When "all the fountains of the great deep" (Gen. 7:11) broke open, the earth's crust split apart all over the world. The underground seas and underwater erupting volcanoes came gushing up through the cracks in the sea floor. At the same time, violent earthquakes caused the mud at the bottom of the sea to mix with the water. Turbulent undersea currents were swirling all over the globe.

Many fish could have lived in buoyant shallow layers of fresh water (lenses) formed on top of the ocean in places where heavy rains fell during the Flood.

It was not an easy time for the creatures that lived in the ocean. Trillions of animals (mostly shellfish) died quickly. Today we see their fossils laid down in thick layers of strata all over the world. In fact, some of the best places to see these fossils is on the top of mountains. Erosion has exposed the fossils and they are easy to find.

Q. *How could the floodwaters cover the tops of the world's highest mountains?*

A. The pre-Flood world was very different than what we see today. The mountains were probably more like rolling foothills, the ground was watered every morning with a mist (Gen. 2:6), and there may have been just one large continent instead of several.

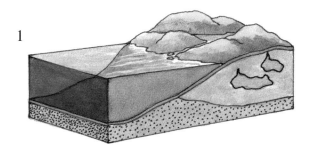

The pre-Flood world was a much gentler place to be than the world we have today. There were probably few temperature extremes (Sahara desert, North Pole) and violent storms (hurricanes, tornadoes, thunder storms.) When Noah and his family walked out of the ark, it was a different world in more ways than they realized at first.

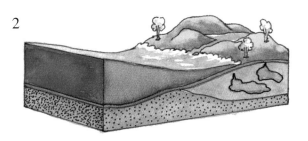

The illustrations show what happened during the Flood.

1. **Pre-Flood**—Rolling hills on land with much of the earth's water in vast underground aquifers (reservoirs).

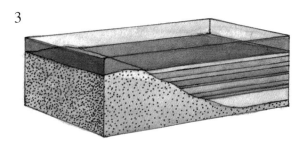

2. **Flood begins**—As the earthquakes release the water in the underground aquifers, the great landmasses begin to sink. Enormous amounts of water (much of it as steam) shoot upward and volcanoes erupt violently. As the landmass sinks, great walls of water rush in from the sea.

3. **During the Flood**—While the Flood continues, vast amounts of sedimentation are laid down on the submerged landmasses. Currents deposit layer after layer of mud on top of each other in rapid sequence.

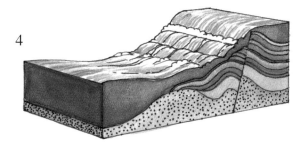

4. **End of Flood**—As the landmasses rise up forming mountains, water pours off them into new seabeds. As the water drains off the land it scours canyons and valleys. The layers are sometimes bent and broken.

5. **The earth today**—As erosion continues we see more and more evidence of a great Flood.

Q. *How did the animals get to different continents separated by vast oceans after the Flood?*

A. When the "fountains of the great deep" burst forth, the temperature of the sea was raised several degrees. The water in the Arctic Ocean was probably warm enough to swim in. This, coupled with the thick layer of volcanic ash in the atmosphere, set up the conditions needed for the Ice Age.

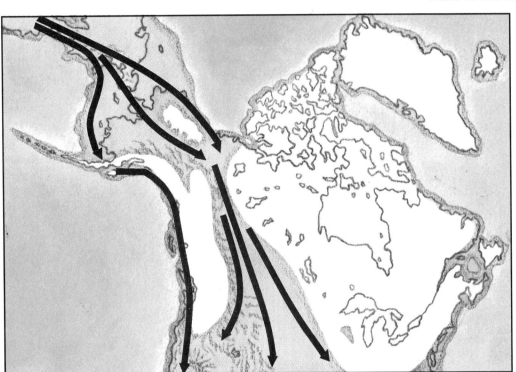

Enormous amounts of moisture evaporated from the ocean and turned into rain and snow over the continents. The ash kept the warm sunlight from melting the snow, and great glaciers and ice sheets formed. As more and more ocean water was trapped on the land, the ocean levels dropped exposing more land. Great "land bridges" joined the continents.

After the Flood, the animals released from the ark rapidly multiplied and migrated across the uninhabited world. To populate the entire world they had to cross from one continent to another. We know that many animals migrated all the way to the tip of South America. Since large animals cannot swim hundreds of miles

at one time, there had to have been land bridges.

A land bridge connected England to mainland Europe. We know this because many Ice Age mammals populated southern England. In addition, fossils have been found at the bottom of the English Channel and the North Sea.

In the far north there lies a shallow area of water in the northeastern Bering Sea, and the Chukchi Sea located between Russia and western Alaska. During the Ice Age, the shallow area formed a land bridge that connected the continents of Asia and North America (see illustration).

Scientists have found the remains of woolly mammoths on several islands in the Bering and Chukchi Seas. Mammoth teeth have been dredged up in the shallow water around Alaska. This is good evidence to prove that a land bridge once connected the continents.

Siberia and northern Alaska were much warmer during the Ice Age than they are today. The animals would have been fairly comfortable as long as they didn't try to cross the glaciers.

After the confusion of languages, the land bridges were the routes the tribes of people used to populate the whole world. Genesis 11:8 says, "So the Lord scattered them abroad from thence upon the face of all the earth." God gave them a command and then enabled them to accomplish His will.

Another possibility for animal migration after the Flood was large mats of trees and other debris, forming "floating islands" that drifted on the oceans for years. These islands could have carried animals from one continent to

Q. *What are fossils and how are they made?*

A. A fossil is a part of an animal or a plant that has been dead a long time—usually thousands of years. In order for a plant or an animal to become a fossil (except under very special circumstances), it must be buried almost immediately after it dies. If an animal dies, and then just lies around on the ground or floats around in the water, it never becomes a fossil.

What happens to a bone, a tooth, or a plant when it becomes a fossil? What usually happens is everything in the bone or plant is replaced, a tiny bit at a time, by minerals dissolved in the water that are in the ground. As water moves through the ground, it carries various kinds of minerals along with it. When the bones and teeth of an animal or parts of a plant buried in the ground, become wet with this water, the mineral in the water replaces all the material in the bone, tooth, or plant, and it becomes hard as a rock. In fact, it is now a rock, but it has almost the exact shape of the bone, tooth, or plant it replaces. It doesn't take millions or even thousands of years for something to become a fossil.

Fossil studies give us evidence of a worldwide catastrophe, such as a flood. A flood would cause sudden burial and provide a natural means of fossilizing bones.

Fossils of dinosaurs have been found in just about every place in the world, from Alaska and Siberia to Antarctica. Sometimes the fossils of many dinosaurs are found all jumbled together in a huge fossil graveyard, just as you would expect if they had been tossed around in a gigantic flood. The illustration shows the stages of fossilization:

1. All land animals not on Noah's ark were drowned in the Flood.
2. The animal was buried rapidly as the Flood deposited soft layers of material that later turned to stone.
3. Fossilization occurred as the animal lay buried deeply beneath Flood sediment.
4. Fossils become exposed as the ground around the animal erodes away.

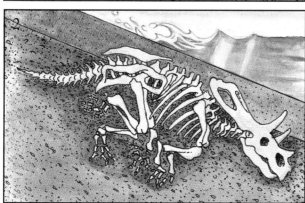

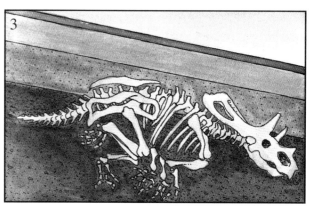

Q. *How many fossils are there?*

A. We have no way to know that, but we do have a good idea of the percentage *ratios of the types* of fossils found.

• Ninety-five percent are marine invertebrates, mainly shallow organisms such as shellfish and coral.

• Of the last 5 percent, 95 percent of those are algae and plant/tree fossils, including trillions of tons of coal.

• Ninety-five percent of the remaining 0.25 percent consists of other invertebrates, including insects.

• The last 0.0125 percent includes all vertebrates, mostly fish, and also includes amphibians, reptiles, dinosaurs, birds, and mammals. Ninety-five percent of the few land vertebrates consist of less than one bone.

Q. *Why are there so few human fossils?*

A. At the time of the Flood there could easily have been well over a million people living on earth, yet it is rare to find fossilized human bones. Why aren't there more discoveries?

• Only a tiny percentage of fossils are land vertebrates (*especially* mammals—that includes humans).

• Mammals bloat when dead and float in water.

• Mammals dismember easily and either quickly disintegrate or are eaten.

• The violent action of the Flood waters would tend to destroy soft-bodied remains.

• Human bodies have a low fossilization potential.

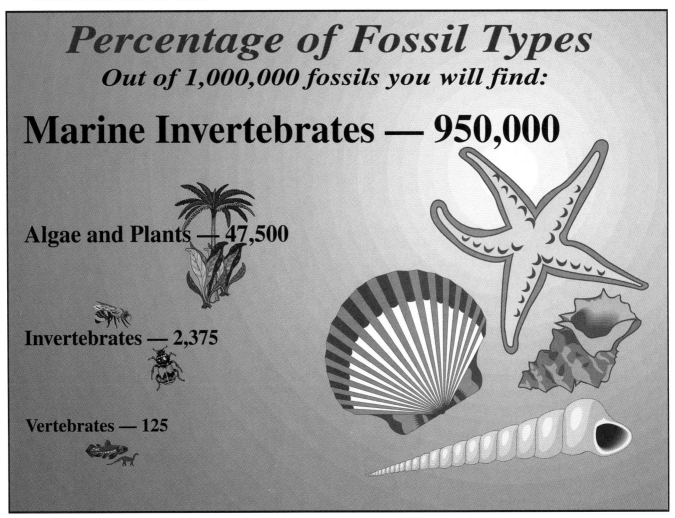

Percentage of Fossil Types
Out of 1,000,000 fossils you will find:

Marine Invertebrates — 950,000

Algae and Plants — 47,500

Invertebrates — 2,375

Vertebrates — 125

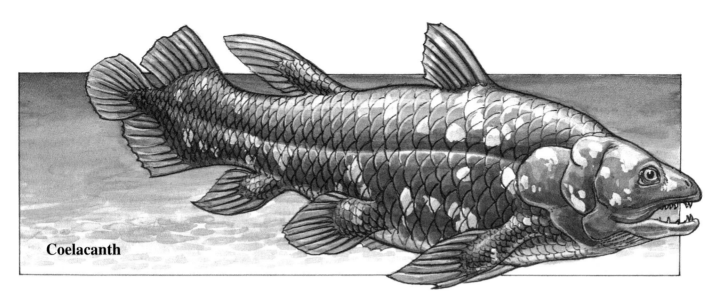

Coelacanth

Q. *Why do some fossils look exactly like animals and plants living today?*

A. What you have described are called "living fossils," plants and animals that are *supposed* to have been extinct for several million years. This presents a real problem for the evolutionist. Did these plants and animals live for millions of years just to die out and suddenly reappear millions of years later?

It would seem a better explanation that the turbulent waters of the Flood buried these plants and animals. A few survived to continue the species until today.

There are many living fossils. Most of them are marine invertebrates, since they're the vast majority of the fossil record. One example is the deep-sea mollusk *Neopilina* that was supposed to be extinct for about 280 million years. Fishermen catch them in their dredging nets off the coasts of Central and South America.

Here are a few others that are fascinating. In 1938 fishermen caught a coelacanth off the coast of South Africa. Not bad for a fish that was supposed to be extinct for 70 million years.

On islands off the coast of New Zealand there's a lizard-like creature called a tuatara. Certain physical characteristics identify it as the only survivor of the order of Rhynchocephalia, or beak-headed reptiles. It supposedly died out 123 million years ago.

Two plants are the *Ginkgo* and *Metasequoia*. Both are alive and doing well. There are many, many more "living fossils."

Living spiders, mites, daddy longlegs, and cockroaches look almost exactly like fossils that are believed by evolutionists to be 380 million years old.

Q. *Just how fast can something become a fossil?*

A. Fossilization depends on several factors. One of the most obvious is the size of the animal or plant. The thicker and denser something is, the longer it will take to fossilize.

An example of *extremely* rapid fossilization is found in northeast Brazil in the Santana Formation. This plateau is 90 miles (150 km) long by 30 miles (50 km) wide and contains millions of specimens of small fish. An article in *Geology Today* by D. M. Martell states, "Gills, muscles, stomachs, and even eggs with yolks have been found. Paleontologists are trained to expect mineral replacement to involve thousands or even millions of years but here lithification [converted to stone] was relatively instantaneous and *fossilization may even have been the cause of death*."[4]

There are fossilized fish with whole fossilized fish (their dinner) in their stomachs. The fossil of one *Ichthyosaurus* is in the middle of giving birth. Something happened to these creatures and it happened *fast!* Fossils like these are found all over the world.

Q. *What are index fossils?*

A. Almost every stratum (singular of strata) of rock contains fossils that seem to be the same type (clams, coral, etc.) Evolutionists look at the stratum these "index" fossils are in and give them the age they believe the stratum is. The problem is, they date the stratum by the fossils found in it. This is called circular reasoning.

Q. *What's the most unusual fossil you've ever heard of?*

A. There are several "strange" fossils around but one of the most interesting is a miner's felt hat from Tasmania. It seems a careless miner left his hat in a mine and when it was discovered 50 years later it was hard as a rock. The minerals in the water that covered the hat had turned to stone.

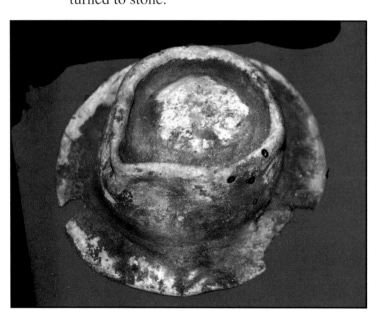

Q. *Doesn't carbon-14 dating prove millions of years?*

A. Carbon-14 dating is not the all-purpose answer many people seem to think it is. It doesn't date rock, but materials that contain carbon and were once living. This dating method seems to be somewhat accurate up to about three thousand years. There are several other dating methods and each serves a different purpose including: rubidium-stron-

tium, uranium-lead, and potassium-argon. Unfortunately, *each* method relies on several *assumptions!* To be truly accurate, *all history* regarding the material to be tested would have to be known.

In Hawaii an 1801 lava flow was dated using the potassium-argon dating method. The results said the lava was almost three million years old. Another series of tests dated 10 samples of lava from Rangitoto (New Zealand) to be between 146,000 and 500,000 years old. Yet, when a sample of wood from *under* the lava was tested, using the carbon-14 method, it gave an age of 225 years (plus or minus 110 years). For more detailed information on dating methods see *The Young Earth* by John Morris.[5]

Q. *What is the Geologic Column?*

A. The Geologic Column is a hypothetical (assumed) column of fossils in various strata with the most ancient life forms at the bottom. Nowhere on earth is there a complete top-to-bottom geologic column. The only place to see one is in a book. In fact, it is not uncommon to find strata with more complex life forms *under* a layer with simpler life forms.

During the Flood, violent earthquakes, undersea landslides (turbidity currents), and incredibly strong currents would have made the water a murky mix of sand, dirt, rocks, uprooted forests, and dead things. As this murky mix settled to the bottom it would have sorted itself into a certain order, not just a random mixture.

Want to try a little experiment? Put some water in a clear container. (Do you have a plastic peanut butter jar?) Then add a big handful each of gravel, sand, and clay. Shake it up thoroughly, set it on a table, and wait for it to settle. What do you see? Layers! This is a simple example of how sedimentary (laid down by moving water) layers, some containing dead animals which became fossils, formed during the Flood.

Genesis Flood Model

Basically, evolution is the belief that over long periods of time one kind of living thing changes (evolves) into another, more advanced kind of living thing. If evolution is true, fossilized plants and animals buried in successive layers of the geologic column should reveal a continuous record of such changes. In fact, *not one example* of one kind evolving into another kind has ever been found!

In the book *Origin by Design*, Harold Coffin presents the Genesis Flood table below. He writes, "If the geological column accurately describes the order in the earth's crust, and the activity of the Genesis flood shaped that crust, we should be able to see parallels between the biblical account of the Flood and the geological column."

The names in the column, rather than mark a several million year period, measure stages of the Flood.

Geological Column	Genesis Flood Narrative		Comparisons and Comments
Precambrian	Pre-Flood		
Cambrian	*Beginning Storm*	Heavy rain (Gen. 7:11–12)	Breakup of earth's crust
			Erosion & deposition of preflood ocean sediments
		Subterranean waters released (Gen.7:11)	Formation of the great Precambrian/Cambrian uncomformity
			Burial of benthonic animals
Ordovician		Rising water (Gen.7:20)	Upward coarse to find grading of sediments
Silurian	*Standing Water*	High water (Gen.7:24)	Deposition of thick shale and limestone
Devonian		Tidal and wave action (Gen.8:3)	Cylothems — rhythmic deposition of sediments
Mississippian		Water covers all land (Gen.7:20)	Formation of coal. Burial of lowland forests, trees of greater density and/or less buoyancy
Pennsylvanian			
Permian		Rain stops, wind starts (Gen.8:1–2)	Crossbedded sandstones
Triassic	*Windstorm*	Mountains rise (Gen.8:5)	Moving continents
Jurassic			Mountain building (tectonic) activities
Cretaceous		Waters start to recede (Gen.8:5)	Major erosion of emerging mountains. Guyots
Paleocene			Burial of reptiles
		Raven & doves released (Gen.8:8–12)	Formation of coal. Burial of upland forests, trees of less density and/or more buoyancy
Eocene			Burial of mammals
			Sediments accumulate along continental margins
Oligocene	*Receding Water*	Water continues to drop (Gen.8:13)	Less dense and less well indurated strata
Miocene			Major volcanic activity
Pliocene		Ark abandoned (Gen.8:14–15)	Localized sediments and valley fills
Pleistocene Recent	Post-Flood		Post-flood erosional re-working of surface sediment Post-flood climatic changes (glaciation)

Harold Coffin, *Origin by Design* (Hagerstown, MA: Review & Herald Publishing Association, 1983).

Q. *How can a creationist and evolutionist look at the same Grand Canyon and draw such different conclusions?*

A. Each one of us has a bias (pre-conceived idea) that determines how we reach conclusions. The creationist, knowing the story of the Flood, looks into the canyon and sees evidence of a massive amount of water gouging out the canyon. The evolutionist, believing in millions and millions of years, has no trouble fitting what he sees into his set of beliefs.

The theory of evolution states that, given enough time, *uniformitarianism* can explain the earth as it is today. Uniformitarianism is the belief that the "present is the key to the past," and that geologic processes (erosion, mountains rising, etc.) have usually proceeded at the same rates that are possible today.

Creationists, however, believe a better explanation for the earth's geology is *catastrophism*—geologic changes made during rapid and catastrophic events. These changes would probably have had long periods of slow and gradual change between them. The Flood of Noah's day would certainly qualify as a catastrophe!

Q. *What evidence supports the creationist's claim?*

A. The Bible says that a worldwide Flood covered the earth for one year. What do we find when we look at geology and the fossil record? Creation speaker, Ken Ham, puts it this way, *"We see billions of dead things—buried in rock layers—laid down by water—all over the world!"*[6]

Q. *Can either creation or evolution be scientifically proven?*

A. For a theory to be considered proven scientifically it must pass three tests: (1) it must be observable, (2) it must be repeatable, and (3) it must be falsifiable (able to test theory and see if it is right or wrong). Since *neither* creation nor evolution can meet any of the three tests they cannot be called a proven science. No one, except God, was present at the beginning. He has given us, in the Bible, a written record of what happened. As creation scientists look at the physical evidence around them—they see that *God's world agrees with what they read in God's Word.*

Q. *Don't the strata in the Grand Canyon show evidence of millions of years?*

A. The truth is exactly the opposite. What you see is evidence of the *rapid* formation of mud layers by energetic flood waters. Evolutionary geologists believe that great amounts of time passed between each layer of strata in Grand Canyon. If this were true, we would find evidence of erosion between the layers.

1. Erosion, even in dry desert areas, is a constant force of nature.

2. The longer an area is exposed, the more erosion occurs.

3. As the new layer of strata is formed it fills in the eroded low places.

The layers of the Grand Canyon are all flat, one on top of the other. There is no evidence of erosion. It is more scientific to think of one major flood leaving many layers of mud, with no time in between.

Interestingly, the almost complete lack of soil between the layers also points to one layer quickly overlaying the one below it.

Erosion is a powerful force of nature. Each year, water and winds erode over 27 billion tons of dirt and rock from the continents and deposit it in the ocean. At this rate, it would take only 15 million years to completely erode all the land above sea level. Yet most of the land is supposed to have been above sea level for hundreds of millions of years.

Q. *Just how did the Grand Canyon form?*

A. Geologist Dr. Steve Austin has spent years studying the Grand Canyon. He has found evidence of enormous lakes that had been contained by great natural dams. These lakes were probably formed when the North American continent rose from the flood waters. He believes when the dams broke, water from these lakes cut through sedimentary layers believed to have been laid down by the Flood.

1

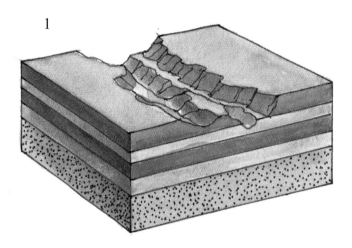

2

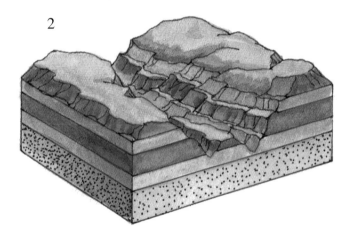

3

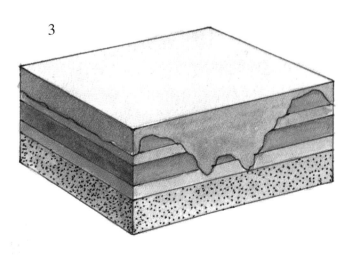

Q. *Are there any "modern" examples of strata forming?*

A. Yes, and a very good example at that! On May 18, 1980, Mount St. Helens (USA) literally blew its top. As volcano eruptions go, this wasn't considered extraordinary. Yet, it was estimated to be 2,500 times the power of the atom bomb that destroyed Hiroshima. A *billion* board feet of timber fell like so many toothpicks. Can you imagine what the world was like with perhaps hundreds of volcanoes going off at once?

When the eruption occurred it melted snow on the mountain, and when the water mixed with volcanic debris it formed huge destructive mud flows. They reached speeds of 90 miles (144 kilometers) an hour picking up sediment, rocks, and ripping up trees. These mud flows laid down enormous amounts of sedimentation.

Then an explosive eruption occurred on March 19, 1982, creating even more mud flows. These eroded large canyons as they scoured the countryside. One of these canyons is now called the "Little Grand Canyon" (photo above) and is a 1/40 scale model of the real one. The new canyon even comes complete with side canyons.

The photo below shows 25 feet (7.5 meters) of stratified deposit laid down on June 12, 1980. It was deposited by pyroclastic (rock material broken into fragments by volcanic action) flows.

Within five years the layers of strata had hardened into solid rock. It doesn't take long to form rock from sediments; it just takes the right conditions.

The bottom photo shows strata made up of coarse and fine sediment. Dr. Steve Austin says of this photo, "It staggers the mind to think how the finest stratification has formed in an event of the violence of a hurricane."[7]

Q. *Are there any more examples of things that seem to be very old, but are really very young?*

A. In 1963, off the coast of Iceland, a huge undersea volcano pushed its way above the waves and became the island of Surtsey. This became a wonderful outdoor "laboratory" to study how quickly change can take place.

Icelandic geologist Sigurdur Thorarinsson wrote in 1964, "Only a few months sufficed for a landscape to be created which was so varied and mature that it was almost beyond belief." Much later, he wrote in a *National Geographic* article, "Despite the extreme youth of the growing island, we now encounter a landscape so varied it is almost beyond belief."[8] This traditionally trained geologist was obviously shocked at what he was seeing firsthand. Things he had been taught would take hundreds or thousands of years to happen were taking place in months or just a few short years.

Q. *I've heard of polystrate trees. What are they?*

A. Polystrate (meaning "many strata") trees are fossil trees that extend through more than one layer of stratum. They are a very dramatic example of strata forming rapidly instead of over millions of years. Any part of a dead tree sticking out of the ground for extended periods of time would decay *long* before it could be buried.

At the Joggins in Nova Scotia, many erect fossil trees are scattered throughout 2,500 feet (760 meters) of geologic strata, through 20 geologic zones. Since these trees had to have been buried faster than it took for them to decay, this implies that the entire formation was deposited in a few years at the most. Yet, evolutionary theory claims that the top strata were deposited millions of years after the bottom strata.

Coal mines are famous for containing polystrate trees. Only in coal mines they are called "kettles" and can be deadly. They appear as rather circular shapes in the mine's roof, and are the bottoms of upright fossil trees. The lower part of the tree, including the roots, are often mined away along with the rest of the coal, leaving only the trunk. If they are not secured with bolts or some other device they can easily detach and fall, crushing the miners below.

Trees are not the only polystrate fossils around. In Oklahoma, Dr. John Morris studied polystrate fossils of reed-like creatures called calamities. These animals were evidently quite fragile because they are usually found only in tiny fragments. For the fossils to still be intact they must have been buried *very* quickly.

At the Green River Formation in Wyoming fossilized catfish are found in abundance, some up to ten inches long. The fact that many have their skin and soft parts preserved point to rapid burial. Often the catfish fossils penetrate multiple millimeter-thick layers. Each layer is *supposed* to represent yearly seasons.

Q. *Surely wood can't petrify quickly.*

A. Petrified wood is wood that has been mineralized (turned to stone) by silica. It's another example of "fossilization" that doesn't take a great deal of time. Australian geologist Dr. Andrew Snelling recently wrote, "Under the right chemical conditions wood can be rapidly petrified by silicification, even at normal temperatures and pressures. . . . The time frame for the formation of the petrified wood within the geological record is totally compatible with the biblical time scale of a recent creation and a subsequent devastating global Flood."[9]

Creation magazine (Sept.-Nov. 1995) gives us a *modern* example of petrified wood that occurred in Venice, Italy. In 1630 the chapel of Santa Maria de Salute was built to celebrate the end of the Plague. "Because Venice is built on water-saturated clay and sand, the chapel was constructed on 180,000 wooden pilings to reinforce the foundations. Even though the chapel is a massive stone block structure, it has remained firm since its construction. How have the wooden pilings lasted over 360 years? They have petrified! The chapel now rests on 'stone pilings'!"

Q. *Doesn't coal take long ages to form?*

A. We have been told that coal takes millions of years to form. Yet, in a laboratory, researchers have made low-quality coal in less that one year. It only takes 11 years to produce coal that is very close to "natural" coal. This was done using materials and conditions easily duplicated in nature. (Diamonds can be made in days and opals in a few months to a few years.)

There are two major theories that explain the natural origin of coal. One states that coal was formed from the burial of plant material right where it grew (autochthonous), and the other says that vegetation drifted or rafted in from somewhere else and was buried (allochthonous). Both theories are compatible with the Genesis Flood. The study of coal is much easier to understand when taken in light of a worldwide flood.

Q. *How long does oil take to form?*

A. Many people think that dinosaurs, buried in sediment, turn into oil in a few million years. But, the chemical makeup of most oil is not what they think. Most experts believe that oil came from oceanic algae. Oil can be made from plant material in hours to days in laboratories using the same conditions found in a great flood.

An article in *Chemical and Engineering News* (May 29, 1972) describes making oil out of cow manure. "The manure was heated at 716 degrees F [380 degrees C], at 2,000 to 5,000 pounds [900 to 2250 kilograms] per square inch for 20 minutes in the presence of carbon monoxide and steam. The product was a heavy oil of excellent heating quality. The yield was about three barrels of oil per ton of manure."[10]

Q. *Is there any other evidence for a young earth?*

A. Yes, there are *many* other evidences that the earth is only thousands and not millions of years old. The two "evidences" following are fascinating and *very* interesting when you analyze the data!

Human Population

The total number of people on earth today is now approaching 6 billion. At its present rate of population growth of about 2 percent per year, it would take only about 1,100 years to reach the present population from one original pair. The 2 percent takes into account disease, famines, plagues, and wars.

But suppose man has been around for one million years, as evolutionists teach. If the present growth rates are typical, there should be about 10^{8600} people alive today! That's 10 with 8,600 zeros following it.

To narrow it down a bit—evolutionary anthropologists say that the Stone Age lasted for at least 100,000 years. During that time the world population of Neanderthal and Cro-magnon men was between one and ten million. All that time they were burying their dead with artifacts (tools, weapons, jewelry, etc.). If this were true there should be about *4 billion* Stone Age skeletons or at least their artifacts. Only a *tiny fraction* of this number has been found!

Sodium (Salt) in the Ocean

Every year rivers and other sources add more than 450 million tons of sodium into the ocean. Only about 27 percent of this sodium manages to get back out of the sea each year.

If the sea didn't have *any* sodium to start with (it probably did), and was *accumulating it at the present rate*, it would reach the current level in *less* than 42 million years. That plays havoc with the *supposed* age of the ocean at three billion years!

But, has the addition of salt to the sea *always* been at the current rate? Sodium is added by rivers (runoff from land), ocean floor sediments, pulverized sediments in glacial ice, volcanic dust, coastal erosion, ground water seepage, and sea floor hydrothermal vents. During and after the Flood, erosion was occurring at an *enormous* rate! No doubt, much of the ocean's present sodium was added then, *drastically* reducing the calculated age! Even the Ice Age would have contributed huge amounts of sodium as the great ice sheets covering the continents melted.

There are other "evidences" (magnetic-field decay, helium in the atmosphere, comets, galaxy speed, etc.) that are totally incompatible with evolutionary timetables. These timetables keep changing as more data is discovered. God's Word, the Bible, has never had to change its timetable of 6,000 to 10,000 years, and has *always* agreed with the world around us!

Q. *The story of Noah and the Flood is all very interesting, but what does it have to do with me?*

A. The story of Noah is not just a fairy tale to be enjoyed and forgotten. These were *real* events happening to *real* people! The world we live in is evidence of a catastrophic Flood. In fact, it is still settling down from the effect of the Flood. Volcanoes, earthquakes, and rising mountains are just a few of the leftover results of the upheaval the earth went through.

The mountain in the photograph is Mt. McKinley, Alaska, and at 20,320 ft. (6,194 m) it is the highest peak in North America. It is also an excellent example of the post-Flood world. Although Alaska is beautiful to look at, it's bitterly cold in winter, severe earthquakes are fairly common, and there are several active volcanos.

Living in the world before the Flood was, in many ways, just like living in our world today. We are once again in a world filled with evil. From the pages of *In the Days of Noah* we can learn much about God and how we should respond to Him in the circumstances we come up against. Here are just a few of the things we can apply to our own lives.

Introduction—God prefers mercy to judgment (Jon. 4:2). God *always* takes care of those who love Him! (Ps. 27:1; Rom. 8:38-39)

God's Covenant with Noah—*Noah believed God!* He was faithful to complete everything that God had instructed him to do.

Noah's Shipyard—Noah planned to build the ark even though it wasn't the "accepted" thing to do. Jabez saw the evil around him, but felt helpless to change it, so he ignored it. Maybe he thought it would just go away.

Dangerous City Streets—This mirrors the violence we see in our cities and towns today— the gangs that feed on violence and liberal courts that often seem to look the other way. A world in rebellion to God makes its own rules.

Construction Site—Even though things aren't happening on our timetable, God is in control, and they're happening on *His* timetable. We can trust God's love for us no matter what happens! God is always there for us when the going gets rough! Sin and death are a part of the world we live in and they affect each one of us. In fact, that is *exactly* why Jesus died on the cross—to defeat sin and death. ***When He rose from the grave on the third day, the victory was complete!***

Noah Preached God's Word—Faithful Noah never gave up telling others about the Lord God and warning them about the judgment to come. Each one listened to the message and thought about the information according to his or her own heart (read Matt. 13:3-8). Their reasons for rejecting Noah's message are many of the same reasons people reject the message of salvation in Jesus Christ today.

Prejudice and Hate—The two women hated Noah and Rebecca because they believed in God and wouldn't fit in with their liberal "anything-goes" society. People who love sin can't stand to be around godly men and women (John 3:20).

Rachel's father loved himself and money more that he loved his daughter. Noah loved his family with the selfless love of a truly godly man.

Ham Is Tempted—Ham was swayed by the people around him. He saw other people having what he thought looked like fun. He was influenced by that and began doing things that were wrong. He thought he wanted to be just like them. But, Ham loved God and when he was confronted with his sin he made a *choice* to leave it. When God created us he gave us a free will. We can *choose* to obey Him, or rebel and "do our own thing."

Wisdom of the Ages—When Adam and Eve sinned by rebelling against God it had seemed like such a small thing. Sin often seems like a small thing, but it is *always* a big thing. **Sin separates us from God—forever!**

Ham knew in his heart how wrong he had been. He wasn't just sorry he had been caught doing something wrong, *he was deeply sorry he had ever done it in the first place!* He realized how much God loved him and he wanted to do the right thing and walk with God!

The Slave Market—Through Adam we are all related! Prejudice has no place in God's world! Every single person is of great value to God! **You are so valuable to God He sent His Son Jesus Christ to die on the cross for you!**

The Wedding—Marriage is ordained (authorized) by God. It is *very* important to Him and is to be between **one man** *and* **one woman**. When God is the head of the home there is love and respect for each other.

Loading the Ark—Ham had struggled for many years to walk with God, but he never gave up. It wasn't easy, but he kept his eyes on God, and listened to his godly family. **He was inside the ark when the judgment came!**

The Animals Arrive—Can you believe all those people saw the animals arrive and *still* didn't believe Noah? Noah called out to them, but they hardened their hearts. They *chose* to believe the temple priests. Whose voice do you listen to?

God Shuts the Door—They had been warned time and time again. Each time they said no to God it seemed to get easier. The time for judgment had come! Only those *inside* the ark would be safe. When God closed the door *He* separated the godly from the ungodly. The ark is a beautiful picture of our salvation in *Jesus Christ—He is our ark! When you belong to Jesus you are already in the ark!* (Rom. 8:1.)

The Wrath of God—*God always does what He says He will do!* No one in their wildest dreams had imagined how terrible the judgment would be! They had been too busy ignoring Noah.

Safe in the Ark—No matter what is going on around us, we are safe in Jesus. *He can be trusted no matter what the circumstances are!* Our view is very limited, but He sees everything and has wonderful plans for our future we know nothing about (Jer. 29:11).

Daily Activities—As the ark pitched and rolled day after day, Noah and his family must have had some pretty scary times. *God had them in His care every single minute!*

Worshiping at God's Altar—It was time to praise and worship God! Noah picked the best animals for the sacrifice to God. He realized there could be no forgiveness of sin without the shedding of blood. That was a picture of what was to come when *Jesus shed His blood on the cross for YOU!* He was *without sin* and yet He took the punishment for your sin upon himself so you could be "saved" from the judgment to come! To receive this salvation admit to yourself and to God that you have sinned, and ask His forgiveness. Then ask Jesus to come into your heart and be your Lord and Saviour (John 3:16). Salvation is a free gift, bought and paid for, but *you must ask for it*. If you said this prayer to God, you are now a member of God's family and safe in Jesus Christ (Rom. 8:14-15)!

Teaching the Next Generation—Can you imagine how wonderful the world today would be if all the fathers had taught their children to worship and love God? The wonderful thing is *you* can tell others about Jesus Christ! He died for the sins of everyone. Tell your family and friends how they, too, can be "safe" in Jesus Christ!

Dedication

The author and illustrators dedicate this book to Dr. Henry M. Morris. His book *The Genesis Flood*, published in 1961 (co-written with John C. Whitcomb), started a renewed worldwide interest in creation science.[11] He then founded the Institute for Creation Research in 1970, and served as its president for 25 years. His recently published *Defender's Study Bible* is the fruit of a life lived in devotion and service to God and His Word.

Acknowledgment

We would like to thank Dr. John Morris, Dr. Larry Vardiman, John Rajca, and Jim Stambaugh who have generously given their time to review this book. Their comments and suggestions have been invaluable. We are grateful to the creation science organizations—the Institute for Creation Research (USA), Answers in Genesis (USA), and Creation Science Foundation (Australia)—for their continuing research and educational projects. The more they learn about the world we live in, the more they find it agrees with God's Word!

Our thanks to Dr. John Baumgartner for the polystrate tree photo on page 75 and Dr. Steve Austin for the photos on pages 72 (bottom) and 74, from "Mount St. Helens: A Slide Collection for Educators."

Recommended Creation Science Reading

High School to Adult:

Austin, Steven, *Grand Canyon: Monument to Catastrophe* (El Cajon, CA: Institute for Creation Research, 1994), 284 p.

Gish, Duane T., *Amazing Story of Creation* (El Cajon, CA: Institute for Creation Research, 1990), 112 p.

Gish, Duane T., *Evolution: The Fossils Still Say No* (El Cajon, CA: Institute for Creation Research, 1995), 391 p.

Ham, Ken, *The Answers Book* (Green Forest, AR: Master Books, 1991), 207 p.

Ham, Ken, *The Lie: Evolution* (Green Forest, AR: Master Books, 1991), 168 p.

Morris, Henry M., *The Biblical Basis for Modern Science* (Grand Rapids, MI: Baker Book House, 1984), 516 p.

Morris, Henry M., *The Genesis Record* (Grand Rapids, MI: Baker Book House, 1976), 716 p.

Morris, Henry M., *Scientific Creationism* (Green Forest, AR: Master Books, 1985), 281 p.

Morris, John D., *The Young Earth* (Green Forest, AR: Master Books, 1994), 208 p.

Whitcomb, John C., and Henry M. Morris, *The Genesis Flood*, (Phillipsburg, NJ: Presbyterian and Reformed Publishing Co., 1961), 518 p.

Children:

Gish, Duane T., *Dinosaurs By Design* (Green Forest, AR: Master Books, 1992), 88 p.

Ham, Ken and Mally, *D is for Dinosaur* (Green Forest, AR: Master Books, 1991), 123 p.

Morris, John D., *Noah's Ark and the Ararat Adventure* (Green Forest, AR: Master Books, 1988), 64 p.

Morris, John D., and Ken Ham, *What Really Happened to the Dinosaurs?* (Green Forest, AR: Master Books, 1990), 32 p.

Oard, Michael and Beverly, *Life in the Great Ice Age* (Green Forest, AR: Master Books, 1993), 72 p.

Parker, Gary, *Dry Bones and Other Fossils* (Green Forest, AR: Master Books, 1995), 80 p.

Endnotes

[1] Henry M. Morris, *The Genesis Record* (Grand Rapids, MI: Baker Book House Co., 1979).

[2] J.A. Thompson, *The Bible and Archaeology* (Grand Rapids, MI: William B. Eerdman Publishing Co., 1972), p. 5.

[3] Paul S. Taylor, *The Great Dinosaur Mystery and the Bible* (Green Forest, AR: Master Books, 1987), p. 46.

[4] D.M. Martell, "The Meducsa Effect: Instantaneous Fossilization," *Geology Today*, vol. 5, no. 6, p. 201–205.

[5] John Morris, *The Young Earth* (Green Forest, AR: Master Books, 1994).

[6] Ken Ham, "What Really Happened to the Dinosaurs?" *Answers in Genesis* video series (Green Forest, AR: Master Books, 1994).

[7] Dr. Steve Austin, "Mt. St. Helens—Geologic Evidence for Catastrophism," *Mount St. Helens: a Slide Collection for Educators* (El Cajon, CA: Geology Education Materials, 1991), p. 4.

[8] Sigurdur Thorarinsson, "Surtsey, the Young Island That Looks Old," *Creation ex nihilo*, Mar–May 1995, vol. 17, no. 2, p. 10-12.

[9] Dr. Andrew Snelling, " 'Instant' Petrified Wood," *Creation ex nihilo*, Sept.–Oct. 1995, vol. 17, no. 4, p. 38–40.

[10] John C. Whitcomb, *The World That Perished* (Grand Rapids, MI: Baker Book House, 1988), p. 124.

[11] John C. Whitcomb and Henry M. Morris, *The Genesis Flood* (Phillipsburg, NJ: P & R Publishing, 1961).